How to Meditate
on the
Living Word

New and Revised Version with Meditation Set Now Combined

Linda Patarello

How to Meditate on the Living Word

ISBN: 978-1-7360325-0-3

Fourth Edition

Copyright © 2014, 2016, 2017, 2020 by Linda Patarello

Editors: DeAnne Ussrey, John Bullock, Daphne Parsekian,
Panagiotis Gavrielatos

Heaven's Treasures

PO Box 1543

Anaheim, CA 92815

TABLE OF CONTENTS

Foreword

L inda Patarello is a former student of mine whom I discovered to be a multi-talented and very gifted individual. She is an accomplished worship leader, pianist, and song writer. In fact, she wrote a song, "All In," from one of the lessons I taught in Bible college, which became the class song for that year. You will also discover by reading this book, as I have, that she is one of the bright new authors of our time.

Linda has a unique way of sharing illustrations and personal examples that both engages and brings truth home to the heart of the reader. This book is a spiritual and practical guide that will help you make meditation a part of your life. As you apply the principles she shares in this book, I am confident it will increase the amount of revelation you receive from God's Word. I highly recommend this book and its author, Linda Patarello, to you.

Greg Mohr

Dean of Education, Charis Bible College, Woodland Park, CO

Part 1 –
How to Meditate

Chapter 1 –
Heart vs. Head Knowledge

Have you ever wondered how some people can speak God's Word with such power that you can sense something is different? You have a sense that they really know beyond a shadow of a doubt what they are talking about. They truly believe it. Yet there are some people who will speak the name of Jesus and it doesn't have any effect on anything or anyone. Still others will speak the name of Jesus with barely a whisper and even the demons themselves shudder and tremble with terror— so much so that they run and hide with frantic fear. That person has a revelation of the name of Jesus. They are completely convinced that His name is deity, the highest name of all names—Jesus spoke with that kind of conviction and faith. Every word was filled with heart knowledge. But of course, He was, and is, the Word.

Any person who has Christ living in them has everything they need inside of them to have the same experience. This is where meditating on the Word of God makes all the difference in the world.

It sets apart those that have only head knowledge but are not yet aware of the living Word. I can attest to this. As a child, I attended a private school. I studied the Word of God, learning prayers and memorizing Scripture. I attended church faithfully, regularly, for years. Yet it was a mere religion to me. Later, in my teen years, I accepted Jesus as my Lord and Savior, but because I was lacking in spiritual revelation, I began to grow weary of the precious Word of God. I was lacking the spiritual revelation that I so desperately needed, the revelation I desperately wished for. Most people are unaware of this need. You can attend church three times a week and still not have a heart knowledge of the living Word. You can die and go to heaven, never realizing the true, rich treasures that are buried and hidden in the Holy Bible.

So really, it's not school alone that will accomplish giving you the revelation of His Word. It's not a theological seminary alone that will cause the living Word to come to life in your heart, although seminary may be a blessing to you. It will be by you yourself planting the seed of His Word in your mind, meditating on it, and renewing your mind with it. This in turn causes it to drop into your heart and grow into a heart knowledge by the power of the Holy Spirit. Then and only then will you have a true revelation of the seed that you have planted. Then you will know that what you have planted is true and not a lie. And it cannot be stolen from you. It's as if a light bulb goes on inside you and you get it. The Holy Spirit, who is your helper, will unveil the Word of God to you in such a way that it will come alive to you, and joy will arise. You will be like a kid who has found buried treasure. A love for His Word will happen and will cause such an appetite that you will crave it and want more and more. You see, many of us have been lied to. We have bought the lie that the Bible is boring, that it is the main book to be ignored and left on a cold, dark shelf collecting inches of dust. Satan (the father of lies) has lied to us and told us (in so many words) that if we have insomnia, the Bible is the book to read for it will surely put us to sleep! But, of course, nothing could be further from the truth.

Meditating on the Word of God, coupled with praying in tongues, will unlock the mysteries of heaven and bring wisdom from above. God our Father is waiting for this to happen to every one of His children.

Walking in the Living Word of God and speaking with the authority of Jesus is where we as His children are supposed to be. This, my friend, should be NORMAL for God's children.

"But his delight is in the law of the LORD; and in his law doth he meditate day and night. And he shall be like a tree planted by the rivers of water, that

bringeth forth his fruit in his season; his leaf also shall not wither, and whatsoever he doeth shall prosper."

Psalm 1:2–3

Chapter 2 –
God's Word Is Alive

"For the Word that God speaks is alive and full of power"

Hebrews 4:12, AMP

It's true that the Bible is an ordinary book with ordinary pages of ordinary paper. Yet there is no other book like it on this earth. No other book carries in it words that are actual seeds that can change circumstances and move mountains. His words are alive and full of the power of God. They will stand, and they will last forever, long after the earth is destroyed. There are no other words that will live on forever.

"Heaven and earth shall pass away, but my words shall not pass away."

Matthew 24:35

If you had a packet of seeds, let's say a new pack of carrot seeds, those seeds can grow, but they will not last forever. At some point, they will perish. The Bible says that God's Word is also seed, but it is incorruptible seed, which means it will not die like the carrot seeds.

"Being born again, not of corruptible seed, but of incorrupt."

1 Peter 1:23

Your new spirit man was reborn by the Word of God. And when you meditate on His Word, that seed is planted in you by thinking on a scripture, a scripture passage, or even a chapter of the Bible. You focus on that throughout your day; you dwell on it, causing that Word to be planted deep in your heart. The more you meditate on that same passage or scripture, the more that it is being watered and is growing—until one day the fruit of the revelation comes, and you begin to understand it. It is inevitable that the Word will grow for it is alive, and it is good seed.

I love to garden and collect lots of different seeds. One summer vacation, while visiting the sequoias in Northern California, I had the utmost privilege of seeing and visiting one of the oldest and tallest trees in the world, "General Sherman." They say it is 2,000 years old. I reached down with joy and held one of the pinecones, which was not huge like you'd expect but actually smaller. To my surprise, it was about two inches long. Suddenly, some seeds fell out of the pinecone into my hands, resembling tiny pieces of raw oatmeal. That was a very special moment. The Lord knows how I enjoy learning about seeds. But even those seeds one day will perish with the earth, as giant as that tree is (the width is something like six cars put together); God's Word does not die. It is more powerful than all seeds, even "General Sherman."

"For the word of God is quick, and powerful, and sharper than any two-edged sword, piercing even to the dividing asunder of soul and spirit, and of the joints and marrow, and is a discerner of the thoughts and intents of the heart."

Hebrews 4:12

The Bible not only describes the Word as seed but also as bread. And bread is what you eat. It should be normal to eat His Word every day. We must have it and be nourished by it as we are nourished by physical food every day. There are too many Christians well-nourished on the outside yet starving spiritually on the inside. Think about it. When you haven't eaten all day (because you were too busy or what have you), your stomach is growling and yelling at you like crazy. "Feed me!" Well, the same is true in the spiritual world. When you have not eaten the Word of God nor spent time in His Word, only living day to day in the natural and tending only to the natural things in life, you feel like you are in a desert, dry and parched. Only you are not sure why. This can last for years for some people. They begin to feel so far away from God. But God hasn't moved, and He hasn't changed. You have. You have not nourished yourself spiritually. You have ignored the signs of spiritual hunger and have gotten busy with the things of this world, not realizing that you will pay a heavy price in doing so. It soon catches up with you.

"Jesus said unto them, I am the bread of life: he that cometh to me shall never hunger; and he that believeth on me shall never thirst."

John 6:35

"But he answered and said, It is written, Man shall not live by bread alone, but by every word that proceedeth out of the mouth of God."

Matthew 4:4

"Jesus said unto them, I am the bread of life: he that cometh to me shall never hunger; and he that believeth on me shall never thirst."

John 6:35

Once you understand that you cannot live without the Word of God, and belief in the power of God's Word, then you will trust it. Then you can begin the wonderful journey of meditating; eating of the nourishing Word of God.

Chapter 3 –
God Gave Us Imagination

"God created man in his own image, in the image of God created he him; male and female created he them."

Genesis 1:27

"And God saw every thing that he had made, and, behold, it was very good."

Genesis 1:31

God used His imagination in order to put life inside of us. He imagined us first, and then He made man. He had to see us in His heart before speaking life into us.

Imagination was given for a good reason. It was so that we could picture good things, keep them in our hearts, speak life into them, and see them come to fruition. Imagination was given to help us meditate on God's living Word—to help us see and envision what God has for us so that we may be blessed and be a blessing to this world.

Imagination is a blessing from God if we use it in the way it was intended to be used. Here are a few scriptures concerning the imagination:

"Keep this forever in the imagination of the thoughts of the heart of thy people, and prepare their heart unto thee."

1 Chronicles 29:18

"God saw that the wickedness of man was great in the earth, and that every imagination of the thoughts of his heart was only evil continually."

Genesis 6:5

The Hebrew word for "imagination," as it is used here, is *yeser* (#3336 Strong's Concordance) meaning form, frame, make, conception, or thing framed.

You can see that it is a framework we are building when we use our imaginations, whether good or bad. The next scripture includes the same Hebrew word, but here it is being used as "mind."

"Thou wilt keep him in perfect peace, whose mind is stayed on thee."

Isaiah 26:3

As you purpose your heart, you can begin to use your imagination to keep your mind stayed on God. Picture Him on His glorious throne. Behold Him in His perfect beauty. Think of His wonderful mercies, and He will keep you in perfect peace. Positive imaginations create positive thoughts. As you begin to dwell on them, they will become planted in your heart, and you will start to produce fruit in your life.

It is definitely a journey as you keep coming back to the Word of God to change your thought life. You reinforce thoughts by coming back to them, so the growth gets stronger and stronger, until one day, revelation knowledge from His Spirit reveals to you the meaning of the Scriptures. What a joyful experience it is when God's Spirit reveals to you the deep wisdom of God's Word. When understanding comes, you will feel like you have just discovered hidden treasure that's been buried for years!

You are being watered by the Word of God as you re- new your mind to His Word. It will change and transform you, as Romans 12:2 (NKJV) states:

"...be transformed by the renewing of your mind, that you may prove what is that good and acceptable and perfect will of God."

Let's look again at 1 Chronicles 29:18, which was mentioned at the beginning of this chapter:

"Keep this forever in the imagination of the thoughts of the heart of thy people, and prepare their heart unto thee."

If you look closely, you can see a pattern or sequence of steps happening. First comes the imagination, which is the pictures being formed in your mind. Then the thoughts form that are built from those pictures, like a blueprint. Those thoughts then drop down into your heart, bringing forth growth to good or evil.

"God saw that the wickedness of man was great in the earth, and that every imagination of the thoughts of his heart was only evil continually."
Genesis 6:5

Our imaginations are a powerful force that can bring forth blessing or cursing in your life. God wants you to use it for the good of others and yourself. Once you learn how it works, your eyes will be opened, and you will need to make a choice. You can either ignore these truths or you can put these principles to work in your life and never let the devil have a field day in your mind again. You see, it's as if through

1. IMAGINATION
2. THOUGHTS
3. HEART

our own ignorance, we have helped him to bury us and mow our lives over with destruction.

"The thief does not come except to steal, and to kill, and to destroy. I have come that they may have life, and that they may have it more abundantly."

John 10:10, NKJV

If the thief is Satan, are you going to help him destroy your life? Have you ever thought that you could be helping him? He is a thief, and he is only out to kill and steal from you and your family. His only aim is to bring destruction and evil to this world. But God is for you, and He is your biggest cheerleader. He only has good plans for your life, but He needs your cooperation in bringing them to pass. You are the only one who can take control of your thoughts. God cannot do this for you. It's your garden. You have control over the imaginations and thoughts that you allow to be planted in it. If you will not discipline yourself to get into the habit of thinking on God's Word, then weeds will start to grow. By weeds, I mean negative thoughts of doubt, fear, worry, and anxiety. The only way to push out bad thoughts from your mind is to put new ones in.

You don't have to think on bad thoughts, but your mind has to be thinking on something. You might as well choose something good. Pull those ugly weeds out, and plant some new, good seeds in your heart today. Water those precious seeds with the Word of God. I promise that if you give yourself to God's Word—if you sincerely give yourself to it with all your heart—you will be changed, and your life will never be the same. So start this journey with God's Word, and you will have endless adventures with your King—the one who loves you as His very own.

Chapter 4 –
How Thoughts Work

In order to explain how thoughts work, let's revisit the topic of seeds. It may be a quick, fleeting thought—a casual thought that comes across your mind—or a pain that hits your body. It might be an evil thought filled with fear or sickness. Any single thought can come to you at any time, but it's up to you to receive it or ward it off with your trusty shield of faith.

"Above all, taking the shield of faith, wherewith ye shall be able to quench all the fiery darts of the wicked."

Ephesians 6:16

The fact that it says, "fiery darts of the wicked," should give you a clue that we have an enemy who is out to destroy us. The enemy is waiting for you to take the bait—or let's just say, he's waiting for you to take the thought. Many people don't realize it, but they take the enemy's thoughts every day, thinking they are their very own, when in reality, they are owning the thoughts of the enemy that are coming against them.

Once you take a thought, his object is to get you to stay there and dwell on it. The longer you do, the easier it is for him to bring destruction upon you. That is how *strongholds* are built, and he knows this all too well.

I would like to share a few scriptures concerning our thoughts. I will also give some of the Hebrew meanings behind these scriptures. This will help bring a clearer understanding regarding strongholds.

"For as he thinketh in his heart, so is he."

Proverbs 23:7

Thinketh in the Hebrew is *shaar: to split or open, to act as a gatekeeper, estimate or think (#8176 Strong's Concordance).*

The gateway to your heart (where the seed grows) is through your mind. If a seed is allowed to stay, it will conceive either good or evil. If it is stopped, it can never be strengthened, framed, and formed. If a bad seed is rejected and you never let it enter your mind in the first place, it can never build a stronghold. First you imagine; then a thought is built.

"God saw that the wickedness of man was great in the earth, and that every imagination of the thoughts of his heart was only evil continually."

Genesis 6:5

"The thoughts of the righteous are right: but the counsels of the wicked are deceit."

Proverbs 12:5

"The thoughts of the wicked are an abomination to the LORD: but the words of the pure are pleasant words."

Proverbs 15:26

"Commit thy works unto the LORD, and thy thoughts shall be established."

Proverbs 16:3

Thoughts, as it is used here, is found 28 times in the Old Testament. In the Hebrew, it is the word *mashashaba: a texture, machine, intention, plan, cunning, curious work, device, imagination, invented purpose, thought* (#4284 *Strong's Concordance).*

In the New Testament, there are many places where Jesus spoke and said, "Take no thought." He also said, "Fear not." He was speaking of either fear, worry, or anxiety.

If you realize what is happening from the very beginning, you can reject the thought quickly and put God's Word in its place. What you are dwelling on today is sure to bring subsequent emotions tomorrow.

Here is an example:

The following thought pops into your mind: "I feel like having some ice cream today." So you take this thought and begin to meditate on a big bowl of ice cream. Thirty minutes later, you get another thought: "Chocolate rocky road! Yummy! Ahh, I can just picture it!" Another hour passes by…"I think my local grocery store has some ice cream on sale today." Pretty soon you hear, "I think I'll just stop and buy some ice cream after work. It's been a long day…I deserve a treat."

Has that ever happened to you before? It could be the same type of scenario played out in so many different ways. Yes, sometimes it's us doing the thinking, but sometimes it is Satan planting thoughts; God will only bring good thoughts because God is only good. Sometimes it's our own flesh. This can happen with any type of temptation. There is nothing new under the sun. People fall for this trick all the time.

In short, thoughts can be the beginning of either greatness or destruction. You only have one mind, and you take it with you wherever you go. It stays with you 24/7—this means you have 1,440 minutes each day to think on something, and no one is twisting your arm inside your brain. You have the freedom to think on whatever it is, anytime you want it, anywhere you want to. You might as well think on something that will be positive and productive, like God's Word.

We have all been born into a sin nature because of Adam's sin:

"Wherefore, as by one man sin entered into the world, and death by sin; and so death passed upon all men, for that all have sinned."

Romans 5:12

This means that you and I were born with a sin nature—or you could say that we were born with a natural tendency to sin. We had to be taught to do right and to use our manners. Do you remember when you were a little child? Your parents might have encouraged you, "Say thank you," or "Say please!" You could have replied, "I don't want to say thank you!" It's easy for people to think negatively or to feel sorry for themselves. Some people would rather frown than smile!

We have to be trained to think on good things instead of bad. It can be done! The Lord will help you, but you must make a final decision to discipline yourself to think on God's Word. Every time your mind wants to sink down and veer off into those same old destructive thoughts, you can bring it back into submission to the Word of God. And the more you meditate, the more victory you will have over a negative thought life!

Here are some other scriptures to meditate on when you want to get into the Word:

"Therefore I say unto you, Take no thought for your life, what ye shall eat, or what ye shall drink; nor yet for your body, what ye shall put on. Is not the life more than meat, and the body than raiment? Behold the fowls of the

air: for they sow not, neither do they reap, nor gather into barns; yet your heavenly Father feedeth them. Are ye not much better than they? Which of you by taking thought can add one cubit unto his stature? And why take ye thought for raiment? Consider the lilies of the field, how they grow; they toil not, neither do they spin: And yet I say unto you, That even Solomon in all his glory was not arrayed like one of these. Wherefore, if God so clothe the grass of the field, which to day is, and to morrow is cast into the oven, shall he not much more clothe you, O ye of little faith? Therefore take no thought, saying, What shall we eat? or, What shall we drink? or, Wherewithal shall we be clothed? (For after all these things do the Gentiles seek) for your heavenly Father knoweth that ye have need of all these things. But seek ye first the kingdom of God, and his righteousness; and all these things shall be added unto you. Take therefore no thought for the morrow: for the morrow shall take thought for the things of itself. Sufficient unto the day is the evil thereof."

Matthew 6:25–34

"But when they deliver you up, take no thought how or what ye shall speak: for it shall be given you in that same hour what ye shall speak."

Matthew 10:19

"But when they shall lead you, and deliver you up, take no thought beforehand what ye shall speak, neither do ye premeditate: but whatsoever shall be given you in that hour, that speak ye: for it is not ye that speak, but the Holy Ghost."

Mark 13:11

"But the angel said unto him, Fear not, Zacharias: for thy prayer is heard; and thy wife Elisabeth shall bear thee a son, and thou shalt call his name John. And the angel said unto her, Fear not, Mary: for thou hast found favour with God."

Luke 1:13, 30

"And the angel said unto them, Fear not: for, behold, I bring you good tidings of great joy, which shall be to all people."

Luke 2:10

"But when Jesus heard it, he answered him, saying, Fear not: believe only, and she shall be made whole."

Luke 8:50

"And when they bring you unto the synagogues, and unto magistrates, and powers, take ye no thought how or what thing ye shall answer, or what ye shall say: And he said unto his disciples, Therefore I say unto you, Take no thought for your life, what ye shall eat; neither for the body, what ye shall put on."

Luke 12:11, 22

"Fear them not therefore: for there is nothing covered, that shall not be revealed; and hid, that shall not be known. What I tell you in darkness, that speak ye in light: and what ye hear in the ear, that preach ye upon the housetops. And fear not them which kill the body, but are not able to kill the soul: but rather fear him which is able to destroy both soul and body in hell. Are not two sparrows sold for a farthing? and one of them shall not fall on the ground without your Father. But the very hairs of your head are all numbered. Fear ye not therefore, ye are of more value than many sparrows."

Matthew 10:26–31

"Fear not, daughter of Sion: behold, thy King cometh, sitting on an ass's colt."

John 12:15

Chapter 5 –
Steps to Meditating

Before I begin to share with you some effective steps for meditating on the Word of God, I would like to share about how I learned how to meditate.

Between the years of 2004–2009, I went through a series of trials where the devil came in and stole just about everything from me. I let him because I was so ignorant about the Word of God and my authority as a believer. I didn't have a clue about how to combat the attacks at the time.

We had a church split, and it was very painful—especially due to the fact that I was on full-time staff as the praise and worship leader. There was so much hurt that I had to deal with that I couldn't bring myself to even sing for three years. I moved on to a large Vineyard church as a church member so that I could take some time to heal. I remember crying during the worship services. God used this large church to help bring healing to me.

During that time, I separated from my husband of 24 years. We were having marital issues and saw our fair share of counselors. It was 2007–2008 when the divorce came. Financial problems started to arise, and I couldn't keep our house by myself due to the circumstances, so I lost it and went into a downward spiral.

Already in my late 40s, I slowly began to get back into the Word of God. I began to listen to excellent Bible teachers, such as Andrew Wommack and Joyce Meyers, but it felt as if I was only at the beginning of my healing. I was still so ignorant of His Word that I woke up depressed every single morning.

I was working at a hospital at the time. Worship leading was what I was used to doing, but I was still not emotionally ready for that yet.

One morning the Lord came and met me. I didn't have a vision nor did I hear Him audibly—it was through my thoughts. I woke up that morning, and I will never forget it as long as I live. I sat on the edge of the bed, so depressed and hopeless. Then I heard these words:

"Are you going to stay this way? You can stay this way if you want to. You can even die this way if you want to. I can't even do anything for you. You have to do it. Only you can make you happy. I can't do it for you because I have already done everything for you. I have given you everything: my promises, my Son, His blood, my love. It's up to you now to respond, and I cannot do this for you. Are you going to stay this way? Or are you going to come over here and get strong in my Word?"

Wow! What an eye opener that was! I said, "Lord, I don't want to stay this way. I don't want to live this way. Okay. I'll do it. I want to get strong in your Word."

This was the turning point in my life. I took it very seriously. I was the only one who could change things in my life. I had all of His promises behind me to back me up and help me, but I was the one who had to put them in me. So with the leading of the Holy Spirit, this is what I did: I bought a little spiral-bound notebook that was small enough to carry around in my pocket or my purse. I began to hunt for scriptures and write them down in my notebook. I knew that what I needed so desperately was God's love. I felt like such a failure. I needed His love to nurse me back to health.

I went on the Internet and found a website where I could research the Scriptures. I put in the words "love, lovingkindness, mercy," and so many scriptures showed up! I began to write down those that spoke specifically about God's love to me from Him. I wasn't ready yet for the scriptures that told me to love others. I needed to know His pure love for me first. I needed to be filled—I was running on empty. All I knew is what God had said to me. His words from that morning rang in my ears: "Only you can do this. Only you can make you happy."

Every day I was writing different scriptures furiously and thinking upon them. I carried around that notebook wherever I went. If I was washing dishes, it was beside me. And as soon as a depressing thought came concerning my circumstances, I rejected it. I refused to go there and would grab a verse and fix my mind on that.

"God is Love…for God so loved the world…" Wait. *"For God so loved me. For God so loved Linda that He gave His only begotten son!"*

No, it wasn't easy, but I was determined. To me, it was a matter of life and death. I stayed in God's Word. After a few months went by, I began to change. My circumstances were the same—they didn't change. But I changed—from the inside out. I noticed it for the first time when I was at work and someone asked me why I was smiling. You see, the majority of workplaces can be so negative, and many people don't even smile, unless it's Friday. But the Word of God was what was changing me and making me smile.

At the same time, I felt like I was in the eye of a storm. The whirling of the storm was going on all around me, yet I had such a peace inside of me. During those days, I had also spent a lot of time worshipping God and crying out before Him. Through praying in tongues, meditating on His Word, and worship, my life changed drastically, and I never went back into depression—living by my feelings and circumstances—again. Yes, the divorce was final. Yes, I had lost my house. But God was with me. His Word was my lifeline. He strengthened me. He rescued me. He gave me a new beginning.

You see, no matter how bad things look in your life, as long as you have God on your side and you put your trust in Him and His Word, you will make it—even if you have to start from scratch like I did. God is a God of restoration. He restores us—that's what He does! Your life is NOT hopeless! You are not doomed to failure. However, if you choose failure and hopelessness, that means that Christ came and died on the cross in vain in your life. You can choose to go that way if you want to, but you don't have to (wink). Choose the path of victory for your life! Now, let's meditate…

Steps to Meditating on God's Word

Whatever it is you need, hunt for and find those scriptures. Write them out, and put them where you can see them often.

Reject the old thoughts, and replace them with new thoughts from the Living Word.

Think on His Word as much as you can—when you wake up, throughout the day, and when you go to sleep.

Speak out the scriptures. Take the words, a few at a time, and fix your mind on them.

As you continue in this process daily, a desire for His Word will begin to grow. That means that the seeds you have been planting are growing!

Chapter 6 –
Let's Meditate Together

In this chapter, we will be making things very practical. I want you to get it. I want you to be able to meditate on your own. All you need is your Bible and the Holy Spirit, assuming that you already have Christ in you! Let's take a New Testament scripture that is very well-known for our first meditation together. Ready? This is how I meditate:

"Therefore if any man be in Christ, he is a new creature: old things are passed away; behold, all things are become new."

2 Corinthians 5:17

Typically, when you see the word "therefore," you need to see what it is there for! We do this by going to the previous verses in the scripture and by following the points that guide us to what the author is trying to tell us. Later, when you get used to meditating, you may be meditating on one whole chapter. For now, since we are only beginning, let's start with just one verse. We can take apart the verse piece by piece:

Your spirit man was born into this world with a fallen nature and was headed for hell. Its natural inclination was to do evil. You had a rebellious nature, which is now gone and passed away forever.

Jesus also suffered on the cross for things that are no longer allowed to be a part of the life of a believer. In Isaiah 53, you can find just some of the things that Jesus took away on the cross in His body for you! Sorrow, grief, sickness, sin, and pain are some of the few that He took care of for us.

Galatians 3 also explains how Jesus was made a curse for us. He was deemed unrecognizable on the cross for our sakes. He took sickness, shame, disease, poverty, sin, and so much more so that we could be permanently set free.

"For he hath made him to be sin for us, who knew no sin; that we might be made the righteousness of God in him."

2 Corinthians 5:21, NKJV

"For you know the grace of our Lord Jesus Christ, that though He was rich, yet for your sakes He became poor, that you through His poverty might become rich."

2 Corinthians 8:9, NKJV

Let's look at the very last phrase of this verse:

"Behold, all things have become new…"

Jesus paid for everything in your spirit, soul, and body. Your spirit man has been made new, and it came from God's Spirit becoming one with yours. *All* things have become new! As soon as you accept Christ as your Savior, you become a new creature. Your body can also be healed by receiving the complete healing that has been purchased for you on the cross. And you can use your faith to receive it—it's yours for the taking through faith in Jesus.

"I am come that they might have life, and that they might have it more abundantly."

John 10:10

Because of God's love, we can experience abundant life on Earth, but it doesn't happen automatically. It is available and already paid for, but you must receive it by faith! This means asking and receiving, knowing that He has already said yes! Abundant life belongs to you as a child of God.

Now let's talk about your soul: your mind, will, and emotions. They have also been promised freedom (abundant life) through the work of Jesus on the cross. We should be the happiest people on Earth. We are God's children, and we don't have to wait until we reach heaven. We can have peace right now—we should be the securest and most content people we know! In order for us to see heaven on Earth, we must first renew our minds. This happens by thinking and living by the Word of God.

"And do not be conformed to this world, but be transformed by the renewing of your mind, that you may prove what is that good and acceptable and perfect will of God."

Romans 12:2

No one can renew your mind for you—even according to the Word of God. God won't make you think His thoughts. He is not a transmitter nor a hard taskmaster like Satan is. God is patient, He's loving, and He gave you a free will to have the ability to follow Him.

"But his delight is in the law of the LORD, and in His law he meditates day and night. He shall be like a tree planted by the rivers of water, that brings forth its fruit in its season, whose leaf also shall not wither; and whatever he does shall prosper."

Psalm 1:2–3

This verse displays the fruit of meditating on the Word of God. When we meditate on the Word day and night, we will be so filled with the Word of God that it will have to come out! That is when bearing fruit becomes easy, and it also becomes a delight.

I would like to give you 2 Corinthians 5:17, the verse we just meditated on, in a couple of different versions. We can read various versions in order to see the scriptures in different ways; it helps us understand their meaning a little bit better. Let's look at these translations and see if they help shed some light on the meaning of the verse:

"Therefore if any person is [ingrafted] in Christ (the Messiah) he is a new creation (a new creature altogether); the old [previous moral and spiritual condition] has passed away. Behold, the fresh and new has come!"

2 Corinthians 5:17

Amplified:

"For if a man is in Christ he becomes a new person altogether—the past is finished and gone, everything has become fresh and new."

2 Corinthians 5:17, Phillips

Wow! One unique translation can truly illuminate our understanding of the Scriptures. I challenge you to look at different translations as you seek to meditate more on the Word, and you will see different perspectives come together to paint a clearer, brighter picture in your understanding of the Word.

Chapter 7 –
Words Spring from Thoughts

There is an old Jewish proverb that says, "My words bring my world." There is much truth here. Thoughts bring life to words, and the way that the cycle of a thought works, as I understand it from God's Word, is as follows:

A picture comes forth from your imagination, which can either be positive or negative. You can choose to dwell on it. You can continue to dwell on it until it begins to sink into your mind. Then you start thinking on that thought...again and again. Once it is planted, it begins to grow; then emotions come into play! Upon maturity, these words bring forth fruit—straight from your lips, from your own tongue. Your belief system has now effectively been built. You saw it; you thought on it. You received it, and then you thought on it some more. Once the Word has been spoken, it can bring forth either life or death. You can speak life or death into anything. You are the one who brings life to it because you give power to the vision to come to pass.

This is how God made us, but He didn't want us to use this power to speak against ourselves. He really desired for us to speak the same Words He spoke. He wanted to teach us His plan for our lives. If we would get on board and see what He has called each and every one of us to do, just think of the possibilities!

"For I know the plans I have for you," declares the LORD, "plans to prosper you and not to harm you, plans to give you hope and a future."

Jeremiah 29:11, NIV

Below are the simple steps of our thought process and also a diagram to help you visualize:

Seeds are presented for you to choose or reject. To accept, you begin the imagination process. To reject, think on God's Word.

Imagination builds the thoughts. Keep repeating the thoughts you have built with your imagination over and over.

These thoughts drop down into your heart and build a root which grows up and out of your mouth. This is the fruit of your lips. You have built a belief system which is now inside of you, and will now come out of your mouth, which will in time come to pass.

"O generation of vipers, how can ye, being evil, speak good things? for out of the abundance of the heart the mouth speaketh."
Matthew 12:34

Our brain sees and learns in pictures. It's like we have a picture dictionary in our brain. We think in pictures. It's how God wired us.

So remember that the progression is this: Imagination helps to form the thoughts that are seeds which then drop down into your heart as you dwell and keep your mind on those thoughts. This is when feelings are present, because you have thought on those imaginations and pictures. Then strong holds are built and grow, as you continue to dwell on them, until they come out of your mouth as words, because you have nurtured them over time, whether they be good or evil. The last thing to follow after the words is the action. The carrying out of those original thoughts.

Imagination helps to form thoughts. Thoughts bring feelings.

Seeds are planted in your heart as you nurture. Growth happens and ultimately comes out of your mouth, fruit that you produced. Lastly, action follows.

Below is a simple picture to help you understand better how it works.

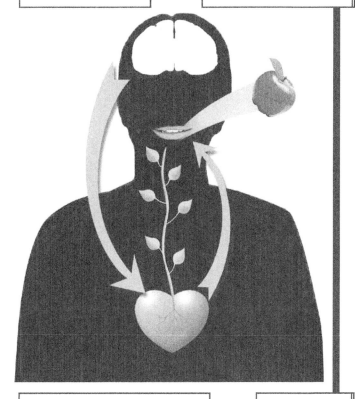

Seeds begin
with imagination
into thoughts
In your mind.

Thoughts are
planted as you give
yourself to them
and dwell on them.

They grow into fruit that
comes out of your lips into
words: death or life. Belief
is set, and action follows.

They spring
to life and
grow strong

"You brood of vipers, how can you, being evil, speak what is good? For the mouth speaks out of that which fills the heart."

Matthew 12:34, NASB

"You brood of vipers, how can you who are evil say anything good? For out of the overflow of the heart the mouth speaks."

Matthew 12:34, TNIV

Once you understand that what will come out of your mouth is whatever is most in you, you will be more aware of what you are putting in your eye and ear gates. It really is crucial what you watch and what you listen to. This is not a game. This is your life and your future. It really is a matter of life and death. Satan is waiting for you to help him destroy your life with your negative words of doubt, fear, and failure.

"A man's belly shall be satisfied with the fruit of his mouth; and with the increase of his lips shall he be filled. Death and life are in the power of the tongue: and they that love it shall eat the fruit thereof."

Proverbs 18:20–21

"Death and life are in the power of the tongue, and they who indulge in it shall eat the fruit of it [for death or life]."

Proverbs 18:21, AMP

"Words satisfy the mind as much as fruit does the stomach; good talk is as gratifying as a good harvest. Words kill, words give life; they're either poison or fruit—you choose."

Proverbs 18:20–21, MSG

Words kill, or words give life; they're either poison or fruit—you choose. Your enemy knows this truth, and that is one reason he is so busy putting evil thoughts in people's minds. Once they take the thought, it is conceived and grows.

He waits and knows it is just a matter of time till it will spring forth to life out of your mouth. I don't want to give him any help. Why should I side with the enemy? I want to be on my King's side, so I must speak what He speaks about me. I will choose to speak words of life and destiny. I will choose to speak words that will heal and bless.

"The soothing tongue is a tree of life, but a perverse tongue crushes the spirit."

Proverbs 15:4, NIV

"A wholesome tongue is a tree of life, but perverseness therein is a breach in the spirit."

Proverbs 15:4, KJ21

"A gentle tongue [with its healing power] is a tree of life, but willful contrariness in it breaks down the spirit."

Proverbs 15:4, AMP

"A pleasant tongue is the tree of life; but the tongue that is unmeasurable, (or unable to be checked,) shall defoul the spirit."

Proverbs 15:4, WYC

Protecting our heart is vital. It is the garden where God's Word grows. In an earthly garden, you would protect your tomatoes against hornworms and other bugs. You would cultivate and aerate the soil, watering, tending and nurturing, being proud to show it to your visitors. You are proud to share the bounty of your harvest. You water it and enjoy it. The same is true with our spiritual garden. Don't allow unwanted thieves that want to intrude and destroy. You have to continually guard and work to keep them out. It will get to the point that you will grow to be spiritually sensitive and know in an instant what is good and what is bad. "No, I will not listen to that. That is doubt, or that is criticism. That is not the right thing to be watching on TV." The Spirit will lead you and your spirit will follow.

Chapter 8 –
Help From the Holy Spirit

"But the Comforter, which is the Holy Ghost, whom the Father will send in my name, he shall teach you all things, and bring all things to your remembrance, whatsoever I have said unto you."

John 14:26

"But the anointing which ye have received of him abideth in you, and ye need not that any man teach you: but as the same anointing teacheth you of all things, and is truth, and is no lie, and even as it hath taught you, ye shall abide in him."

1 John 2:27

The Holy Spirit is a gift. The Father sent Him to us. We are not to be afraid of Him. God is love. Why would He send you anything that would possibly frighten you?

When people don't understand something, they may choose to close the door and not listen, not learn. I would like to speak to those of you who feel that way right now. What if you were wrong? What if this really was from God? We know that God is a supernatural being. But you and I were made in His image, so I believe that makes us supernatural as well. I don't want to miss anything God has for me. I trust Him. I know He loves me and that He has only the best intentions for me. Healing is meant to flow through me to others. The power of God was meant to flow through me. It should be as natural as it was with Jesus. He gave and showed mercy to all.

"But if the Spirit of him that raised up Jesus from the dead dwell in you, he that raised up Christ from the dead shall also quicken your mortal bodies by his Spirit that dwelleth in you."

Romans 8:11

"And hope maketh not ashamed; because the love of God is shed abroad in our hearts by the Holy Ghost which is given unto us."

Romans 5:5

"But ye, beloved, building up yourselves on your most holy faith, praying in the Holy Ghost."

Jude 20

When we pray in tongues, we are building ourselves up. Or you could say we are charging our spiritual batteries. I have made a habit of this. It has now become like an instant reflex, you might say. I will be driving down the street and not even realize that I am praying in tongues. It is under my control. I can stop and start anytime I want to. Just like with my own English language, I can whisper or shout when I want. Well, I know that speaking in tongues helps me to understand the Word better. If, when I pray in tongues, my spirit is praying mysteries to God (1 Cor. 14:2), then I trust that that is the wisdom from above. Wisdom on how to pray and wisdom on how to understand the Scriptures is vital for you and me to learn. And Jesus did not leave us alone. He loved us so much that He wanted us taken care of.

"Howbeit when he, the Spirit of truth, is come, he will guide you into all truth: for he shall not speak of himself; but whatsoever he shall hear, that shall he speak: and he will shew you things to come."

John 16:13

"But when the Friend comes, the Spirit of the Truth, he will take you by the hand and guide you into all the truth there is. He won't draw attention to himself, but will make sense out of what is about to happen and, indeed, out of all that I have done and said. He will honor me; he will take from me and deliver it to you. Everything the Father has is also mine."

John 16:13, MSG

What I can tell you is from my experience. As I began to meditate as a lifestyle, as well as pray in tongues, I began to notice my meditation on the Scriptures became more fulfilling. For instance, I would think on a scripture and tear it apart a phrase at a time, and then another scripture would come to mind that fit, as if a puzzle were being put together. I realized it was the Holy Spirit who was helping me. It was fantastically amazing. Sometimes I would see the whole puzzle put together as if it were a picture. It became fun to meditate. As I would ponder on different scriptures that fit together, I would ask the Holy Spirit, "Well, what about this?" And He would answer and show me. This has happened many times, and no one can convince me that He is not real. He has comforted me often and will do the same for you. But you must remember to come to Him for comfort.

We are not on this earth alone. He is with us. And the Holy Spirit will help you where you are weak (Romans 8:26–28). Lean on Him. He loves it when we come to Him for help. That is what He is there for. You can never say that you are alone. Why, you have the angels with you that far outweigh the demons, which are defeated. If God be for us, who can succeed against us?

Chapter 9 –
You Can Love God's Word

I shall be honest and tell you that I was one of those who thought that the Bible was a boring book, but that was because of ignorance and lack of meditating on it. It was not until my divorce and through my learning how to meditate on the Bible that this changed.

Whatever you spend the most time with is where your heart will be. If you spend time with evil, your heart will lean unto evil.

"For where your treasure is, there will your heart be also."

Matthew 6:21

"Your heart will always be where your treasure is."

Matthew 6:21, CEV

"A good man out of the good treasure of his heart bringeth forth that which is good; and an evil man out of the evil treasure of his heart bringeth forth that which is evil: for of the abundance of the heart his mouth speaketh."

Luke 6:45

You will crave it, and that is where your comfort zone will be. It can even be a very evil, bad place that is your comfort zone. Confusion can even be one's comfort zone. I have been in environments before where there was lots of shouting, and noise with no peace. But this was a comfort zone for those there. They were used to this. If they were put in a quiet and peaceful environment, they might feel out of place. Some might even create confusion just because they want to feel peace again, although this is a false peace.

Just as it takes time to create a new habit, it will take time for the Word to become your new comfort zone. That's okay. I encourage you to give yourself to the Word of God. When it happened to me, I would wake up in the middle of the night with a scripture on my mind. When I would wake up, immediately another scripture would also be on my mind to comfort me. In the morning, I would write down a scripture to take with me to work in my pocket. It kept me through the day. I would get to work and park in the large parking structure. It would be a bit of a walk to my small office cubicle, but the walk was glorious while passing through manicured lawns and tall, old shady trees. I would look up and see the sun's rays streaming through the branches. It would cause me to worship Jesus, and then scriptures would pour through my mind like water, refreshing me and causing me even to worship and cry. I refused to think about the problems that filled my mind. I shut the door on thoughts of worry and negativity, not allowing any thoughts except comforting ones. These were the only thoughts I would leave room for. Whenever something started to rock my world, I ran to the Word. Pretty soon it was my lifeline. It fed me like food. It caused me to rejoice in the mercy of God for me. Pretty soon it began to speak to me. I didn't realize that the Holy Spirit was encouraging me and comforting me.

The next thing I knew, I fell in love with His Word. I wanted to be with God. I wanted to spend time with Him. Yes, I listened to teaching CDs much of the time. But now I spent more time before the Lord in quiet, meditating on His Word. He began to unravel His Word. I began to understand it as if a light bulb went on in my heart. This is called revelation knowledge, or a heart knowledge, which is not just a head knowledge, where you may read and even memorize a verse of scripture. Anyone can do that. But it takes the Holy Spirit to unveil His Word to you and me. We cannot do it alone. It is a gift the Spirit allows us.

King David is a great example of someone who loved God's Word. If you read through Psalm 119, you will find many helpful scriptures. Here are a few:

Verse 16: *"I will delight myself in thy statutes: I will not forget thy word."*

Verse 23–24: *"But thy servant did meditate in thy statutes. Thy testimonies also are my delight and my counselors."*

Verse 47: *"And I will delight myself in thy commandments, which I have loved."*

Verse 72: *"The law of thy mouth is better unto me than thou- sands of gold and silver."*

Verse 97: *"O how love I thy law! it is my meditation all the day."*

Verse 103: *"How sweet are thy words unto my taste! Yea, sweeter than honey to my mouth!"*

Verse 162: *"I rejoice at thy word, as one that findeth great spoil."*

Verse 167: *"My soul hath kept thy testimonies; and I love them exceedingly."*

When you have truly given yourself to His Word and think and ponder on it day and night, which, by the way, can be done at work or wherever you are as long as you can think or concentrate, then you will be like David. You will fall in love with the Bible. It will become sweeter than honey and worth more than gold or silver. It will become your wisdom and will flow out of your mouth. You actually won't be able to stop it. It will be so much a part of you, so deep within you, that you will be speaking over yourself, over others. You will become a tree to bring shade and refreshment to everyone you meet. You are now a vessel of God's, a blessing indeed.

Chapter 10 –
Receive Jesus as Your Savior

Y ou have a free choice to receive Jesus Christ as your Lord and
Savior. Know that this is the most important decision you'll ever
make!

*"If thou shalt confess with thy mouth the Lord Jesus, and shalt believe in
thine heart that God hath raised him from the dead, thou shalt be saved. For
with the heart man believeth unto righteousness; and with the mouth
confession is made unto salvation."*

Romans 10:9–10

"For whosoever shall call upon the name of the Lord shall be saved."

Romans 10:14

*"For by grace are ye saved through faith; and that not of your- selves: it is
the gift of God."*

Ephesians 2:8

Like a child, just believe and receive. Jesus already did all the work.
It's so much easier to come to God when you understand that He is a
good God who loves you no matter what. He accepts you right now
as you are. You don't have to clean up first—Jesus will do that for
you.

*If you would like to receive Jesus Christ into your heart, all
you have to do is pray this simple prayer:*

"Lord Jesus, I confess that you are my Lord and Savior. I believe in my heart that God raised you from the dead. By faith in your Word, I receive salvation now. I give you my life. Thank you for saving me!"

If you meant that with your heart, you are now saved! Remember, it has nothing to do with your feelings, only the decision you've made. Now that you are born again, you are brand new!

"Therefore if any man be in Christ, he is a new creature: old things are passed away; behold, all things are become new."

2 Corinthians 5:17

Chapter 11 –
Receive the Holy Spirit

W hen Jesus rose again to be at the right hand of the Father, He didn't want us to be alone. He told the disciples to wait—that the Father would send a Comforter to be with them, a helper. As you read the Scriptures and see for yourself that He is from God, you can take comfort that this is a blessing. He only wants the best for us, and we need not be afraid of anything given by God, because He loves us. The Holy Spirit is a gift from God.

"But when the Comforter is come, whom I will send unto you from the Father, even the Spirit of truth."

John 15:26

"Howbeit when he, the Spirit of truth, is come, he will guide you into all truth: for he shall not speak of himself; but whatsoever he shall hear, that shall he speak: and he will shew you things to come."

John 16:13

"But ye shall receive power, after that the Holy Ghost is come upon you: and ye shall be witnesses unto me both in Jerusalem, and in all Judaea, and in Samaria, and unto the uttermost part of the earth."

Acts 1:8

The Word explains how they were filled:

"And they were all filled with the Holy Ghost, and began to speak with other tongues, as the Spirit gave them utterance."
Acts 2:4

And you must know that the Holy Spirit is still for us today because:

"Jesus Christ [is] the same yesterday, and to day, and for ever."
Hebrews 13:8

"For every one that asketh receiveth; and he that seeketh findeth; and to him that knocketh it shall be opened. If ye then...know how to give good gifts unto your children: how much more shall your heavenly. Father give the Holy Spirit to them that ask him?"
Luke 11:10, 13

If you would like to receive the precious Holy Spirit, all you have to do is ask, believe, and receive. Just pray this simple prayer:

"Father, I recognize my need for your power to live this new born-again life. Fill me with your Holy Spirit. By faith, I receive Him right now! Thank you for baptizing me. Holy Spirit, you are welcome in my life in the name of Jesus."

It's that simple. The Holy Spirit is a gentleman and won't come uninvited. You are filled with God's supernatural power. Some syllables from a language you don't recognize will rise up from your heart to your mouth, and as you speak them out loud by faith, you're releasing God's power from within and building yourself up in the Spirit. No man understands these words, but God does. You are speaking mysteries to God. You're speaking spirit words to His spirit. You are speaking the wisdom of God in your life. Don't try to figure it out; remember, it is in the spirit, not in the mind.

He will help you to pray in tongues, but it's your tongue. The Holy Spirit won't force you. As you worship and give Him your tongue, then begin to speak sounds, not English or your own native tongue. He will form them into words. Trust Him to help you. And forget about thinking that you're making it up.

You may only have one word at first.

Practice, just as a child learns to speak his language by starting with just a word or two. Make a habit of praying in tongues. You may think, *I'm only praying one word.* But in God's eyes, according to His Word, you are speaking mysteries. You are speaking the wisdom of God for your life and for others. It will bless you.

"For he that speaketh in an unknown tongue speaketh not unto men, but unto God: for no man understandeth him; howbeit in the spirit he speaketh mysteries.

1 Corinthians 14:2

"He that speaketh in an unknown tongue edifieth himself."

1 Corinthians 14:4

"For if I pray in an unknown tong

1 Corinthians 14:14

You can do this whenever and wherever you like. You can also pray for your loved ones and for the many situations in which you need wisdom. It doesn't really matter whether you felt anything or not when you prayed to receive the Lord and His Spirit. If you believed in your heart that you received, then God's Word promises you did. What a wonderful new journey you have embarked on. Seek the Lord, and He will show Himself real to you.

Don't wait to enjoy God's promises until you finally reach heaven. Live today as He planned for you to live. Enjoy His promises, His presence, His love, and His sweet fellowship and conversation. You will see that there is nothing that can compare to it, nothing—no one and no thing. No amount of money, no fame, and no material goods can satisfy that craving in your heart, that perpetual longing that only Jesus can fill, that only the love of the Father can meet. Take it, child. It's yours.

"I am the root and the offspring of David, and the bright and morning star. And the Spirit and the bride say, Come. And let him that heareth say, Come. And let him that is athirst come. And whosoever will, let him take the water of life freely."

Rev. 22:16b–17

Part 2 –
Meditating on the Scriptures

Meditations 1 –
I Am Free

Your victory has been paid for by Jesus Christ, but we live in a world where there is evil. While you live here, every single day you need to hold your shield of faith up. We have an enemy who is out to destroy us, to lie to us, telling us we don't have the victory. The fight, then, is for your mind, so every single day you must live by faith, which means you don't let down your shield no matter what. You believe the word of truth and that He has already given us the victory. You and I must take the land and enforce that victory!

"Wherefore take unto you the whole armour of God, that ye may be able to withstand in the evil day, and having done all, to stand."

Ephesians 6:13

After you have put on the whole armor of God, you are to stand firmly in your place. When an army stands their ground, they hold their position and don't let the enemy through. As a Christian, you are called to stand on God's Word. We do not let go of God's Word; we choose what He says above all else. Just like a bull dog holds tight and doesn't let go, we are to hold on to the promises of God.

"Now the just shall live by faith."

Hebrews 10:38

We have been given five senses to help us in this world, but they were not meant to lead us or to take over in our lives. God is a God of faith and He lives by faith; He speaks of things that are not as though they were. We are His children, and we should live the same way. To live by faith means that faith is a priority in your life above feelings and above circumstances.

"And the devil that deceived them was cast into the lake of fire and brimstone, where the beast and the false prophet are, and shall be tormented day and night for ever and ever."

Revelation 20:10

Satan is the deceiver and the father of lies. He has brought destruction to millions of people; he has murdered children and anyone else who stood in his way. There is coming a day when God is going to cast the devil into the lake of fire, and he shall be tormented day and night forever and ever. He has already been defeated by Jesus but has not yet been captured to be thrown into the lake of fire. I believe many millions of believers will be mourning forthe souls that did not choose Jesus, those that will be destined for hell. But those same millions of Christians will be cheering to see Satan thrown into the lake of fire, where he belongs.

"For this purpose the Son of God was manifested, that he might destroy the works of the devil."

1 John 3:8

Jesus is God come in the flesh. Jesus, the Son of God, came in boldness to destroy all of the works of the devil. When He was on the earth, anywhere there was sickness and disease or demons wreaking havoc in people's lives He showed mercy by reaching out to heal and bring freedom. He had the authority. Satan is a thief (John 10:10) and comes to steal, kill, and destroy. This should be our same attitude wherever we are. We should hate evil and destruction and take our authority that has been given to us. We should not stand idly by and watch. When we have His Spirit living in us, we are equipped to break the bonds and heal the sick.

"And having spoiled principalities and powers, he made a shew of them openly, triumphing over them in it."

Colossians 2:15

"[God] disarmed the principalities and powers that were ranged against us and made a bold display and public example of them, in triumphing over them in Him and in it [the cross]."

Colossians 2:15, Amplified

The Lord disarmed the principalities and powers. To disarm means to take the weapons away. Now they have no weapons, no power—only deceit. He not only disarmed them but He made a spectacle of them, a bold display for all to see. Those in hell saw. The angels and the spirit realm must have seen. Perhaps those who had passed away were able to see. He didn't do this act in a shy way, but He triumphed instead. All the credit that we give the enemy is a shame. We let ourselves sometimes believe that he is stronger than God. What a lie that is.

"And ye shall know the truth, and the truth shall make you free."

John 8:32

There is truth, and there is the lie. Jesus is the truth, the way, and the life. Jesus brought the truth. He didn't come to condemn the world; He came to save it (John 3:17).

Once your eyes are opened to the truth and you see with your heart, the truth makes you free. To be free is a wonderful thing.

Freedom comes from God. He has the power to make you free. He wants men free to know the truth. Bondage comes from Satan. Religion can cause bondage, but the Word of God can set us free.

"If the Son therefore shall make you free, ye shall be free indeed."
John 8:36

In Mark 5, we read about the man who dwelled among the tombs with an unclean spirit. Men would often bind him with chains to control him, but he would rip them off and no one could control him. He was being controlled, instead, by Satan and was in terrible bondage to him. The Bible says that always, night and day, he was in the mountains crying and cutting himself with stones. There was a legion of demons inside of him. He was trapped as if in prison. This is how he lived until Jesus came and commanded, "Come out of the man." After it was all said and done, the man was found sitting, clothed, and in his right mind. Only Jesus can do this for good. When Jesus makes you free, you are completely free for good. You will never be trapped again, unless you let it happen. His Word will keep you free.

"Being justified freely by his grace through the redemption that is in Christ Jesus:"
Romans 3:24

You could say justified means "just as if I'd never sinned." How can this be? One would say, "Don't I have to earn this?" No. This is a gift.

It is by the grace of God. You can never buy it. Your redemption has been paid for. A high price has been paid by the Son of God, Jesus Christ. It is yours for the taking. Just receive your redemption. You've been redeemed by the blood of the lamb. Through His sacrifice on the cross, your redemption is here today.

"But not as the offence, so also is the free gift. For if through the offence of one many be dead, much more the grace of God, and the gift by grace, which is by one man, Jesus Christ, hath abounded unto many."

Romans 5:1

The wages of sin is death. Adam sinned and brought death to all. We were then all born into the sin nature because of Adam. The wages of our sin is death, but the free gift of righteousness is different because it is not earned. It is given. You as a receiver don't do anything but receive when a gift is given to you. The one that gives the gift is responsible for choosing and purchasing it. It is by God's grace that righteousness is given; the offense of Adam abounded unto all, but His free gift has also been given unto all who will receive it.

"For he that is dead is freed from sin."

Romans 6:7

When Jesus died on the cross, He took all of our sins—past, present, and future—with Him. When He took our sins, He paid for us to have His life. And when we received Him, His Spirit came to live inside of us. Our old sin nature died on the cross with Jesus. Romans 8:10 says, "And if Christ be in you, the body is dead because of sin; but the Spirit is life because of righteousness." So if we are alive with Him, we have also died with Him. Our sins, our past, our grief and sorrows, and even our sicknesses and bondages are all gone. You could say it this way: Now that my sin nature has died with Jesus, I am freed from sin, I am freed from bondage, and I am freed from sickness.

"Being then made free from sin, ye became the servants of righteousness."

Romans 6:18

If I am free and the devil is defeated, then I can choose, with my free will, to serve God with my body, my will, my mind, and my emotions. No one has a noose around my neck any longer. No one is twisting my arm. I am free to choose life. I am free to choose the way I want to live from now on.

"But now being made free from sin, and become servants to God, ye have your fruit unto holiness, and the end everlasting life."

Romans 6:2

Our fruit used to be bent toward evil, but now we are freed from sin. We have become a servant of God and unto God. We now have new fruit unto holiness, and it will just keep getting better—a new life, a clean life—all the way into the forever with the Lord with life everlasting. Peace and freedom forever and ever. It is mine because I am loved by Jesus. I am loved by the Holy Spirit. I am greatly loved by my real heavenly Father (Matthew 23:9).

"For the law of the Spirit of life in Christ Jesus hath made me free from the law of sin and death."

Romans 8:2

Now that you are "in Christ," the law of the Spirit of life in Christ Jesus has made you free. You are not under the law of sin and death any longer. The law of sin and death brought guilt and condemnation. Being under the law is always having the mirror in front of you, where you are forced to see your mistakes, sins, and weaknesses. When Jesus died on the cross, He fulfilled the law. You are under a new law now that is full of God's life, peace, and freedom from bondage. Grace reigns. You have peace with God, and you are His own. You are accepted in the beloved. You are loved. When you know you are loved, you want to do right and please God. You live by leaning on His strength and not your own any longer. He supplies all that you need.

"He that spared not his own Son, but delivered him up for us all, how shall he not with him also freely give us all things?"

Romans 8:32

God the Father did not spare Jesus. He did not hold on to Him. He gave Him for us. God SO loved the world that He gave His only begotten Son. The true test of a real giver is when they are willing to part with something that is most valuable to them. There are times when God will ask us to give something that we have treasured for a long time. He'll say to us, "Give that to so and so." We'll say, "No, Lord, you don't mean that, do you?"

Once we surrender to this thought and obey, we will have peace, but it's always a hard thing to do in the beginning. But it is good to obey and let go. When we do, we experience, in a tiny way, what God felt when He gave His most prized possession, His Son Jesus. When we give up something, we want to know that the one who receives it will take care of it. God delivered Him up to take the sins of the whole world, to carry all of our grief and sorrows, to be made sin and to take all of our diseases. The pain in God's heart to bear this must have been tremendous, but He was willing. If God freely gave His own Son, shall He not also freely give us ALL things? All the promises of God in Him are yes and amen (2 Corinthians 1:20).

"For whosoever shall call upon the name of the Lord shall be saved."

Romans 10:13

This is a very short and simple verse, and yet even from the simplest verses you can glean a lot of wisdom. Taking a few words at a time, we focus on the beginning "whosoever." This can be anyone, regardless of your ethnicity, your upbringing, or your religion; regardless of one's fame or fortune, political status, or royal standing. A child, or even a homeless person, can be a whosoever. As long as this whosoever can call upon the name of the Lord, they can be saved. It does not specify the place even. One need not be in any large cathedral to call upon the name of Jesus. Jesus is the one who saves, and we are the ones who call. Anywhere, anytime is good. "Shall be saved" is the outcome. They shall be saved from hell and eternal damnation, from darkness and bondage.

"Stand fast therefore in the liberty wherewith Christ has made us free, and be not entangled again with the yoke of bondage."

Galatians 5:1

If you were set free from a prison, would you want to go back again? We must hold on to our freedom. Every day we can choose life or death; that is up to us. He is telling us to stand fast and hold on to our liberty. Choose it every day! Stay there. He paid a heavy price to set us free; why would we want to go back? Don't get tangled again in that trap. Old things are passed away, and you are not a loser anymore. Get the right perspective. You are a child of God. You have been delivered from the power of darkness.

"Christ hath redeemed us from the curse of the law, being made a curse for us: for it is written, cursed is every one that hangeth on a tree:"

Galatians 3:13

Deuteronomy 28 speaks about the curses, but Jesus became the curse for us. It is good, however, to read those so you can see what He took and what you have been redeemed from. In the Old Testament, if you were hung on the cross, you were cursed; it was common to have that done outside of the city gates. We were meant to go to hell, for we have all sinned and fallen short of the glory of God, but He did it for us.

"For as much as ye know that ye were not redeemed with corruptible things, as silver and gold..."

1 Peter 1:18

It wasn't silver or gold that saved us, but it was something much better and surer. If silver and gold are corruptible, that means they can be destroyed—they can and will be corrupted one day. We were redeemed by the blood of the lamb (Colossians 1:14). The blood of Jesus is holy and pure, perfect and spotless. His blood was the perfect offering, and it was incorruptible. This means our redemption is forever and will never end.

"And they sung a new song, saying, Thou art worthy to take the book, and to open the seals thereof: for thou wast slain, and hast redeemed us to God by thy blood out of every kindred, and tongue, and people, and nation;"

Revelation 5:9

It is the four beasts and twenty-four elders that sing a new song, and this verse then explains what the words of the song are. Picture this: Verse 8 states that they each have harps. They are gratefully singing a most beautiful heavenly song, with honor and reverence," Thou art worthy to take the book, and to open the seals thereof: for thou wast slain, and hast redeemed us to God by thy blood out of every kindred, and tongue, and people, and nation…." Only He is worthy. Only He redeemed us. Every one of us has been paid for, if they would only come, believe, and receive what He has done.

"Let the redeemed of the LORD say so, whom he hath redeemed from the hand of the enemy;"

Psalm 107:2

We shouldn't hide it or be ashamed of it. We should speak it to ourselves and anyone who will listen. The hand of the enemy was too strong for us. We couldn't save ourselves. He rescued us. Jesus is our champion.

"But now thus saith the LORD that created thee, O Jacob, and he that formed thee, O Israel, Fear not: for I have redeemed thee, I have called thee by thy name; thou art mine."

Isaiah 43:1

If we are in Christ, we are grafted into His family. He created us, and it is God who formed us. We should not fear, for it is He who has redeemed us. He made us, and He rescued us; He bought us back. He has called us each by name. He knows us. We belong to Him, but not in a taskmaster sort of way. Remember that God is love and everything He does comes through the motivation of love. When no one wanted us, He did. When we have suffered rejection, He will never reject us. When some have left us, He will never leave us. He loves you. He will always want you and is glad to call you His own.

"I have blotted out, as a thick cloud, thy transgressions, and, as a cloud, thy sins: return unto me; for I have redeemed thee."

Isaiah 44:22

Your wrongdoings and your rebellion used to be as a thick cloud. Imagine a thick black cloud in the sky, dark and shadowing the land, so threatening as it moves. With one wave of His hand, He wipes it away, and the sky is blue and clear again; the bright sun is shining, and you again feel its warmth. He has erased your sins. He doesn't see them. He has cleared the way. He did it for you because you were unable to. And then He brings the invitation: "Return to me. For I have redeemed you." You see, He wants you. He is waiting for you to make the choice.

"Sing, O ye heavens; for the LORD hath done it: shout, ye lower parts of the earth: break forth into singing, ye mountains, O forest, and every tree therein: for the LORD hath redeemed Jacob, and glorified himself in Israel."

Isaiah 44:23

So poetic is the redemption of man. All the heavens are called to sing! The valleys and the mountains and all of creation are called to break forth into song! Every tree of the forest and every green tree of the whole earth come and shout, come and sing! God has glorified Himself; He has glorified love. He has redeemed Jacob. And we that are in Christ are also included in Jacob. He has redeemed us and purchased us back rightfully through his Son. All the wrath for sin was placed on Jesus. Now we can sing the song of freedom! There are songs from one's own country that declare emancipation. But they cannot touch this heavenly song of redemption!

"Therefore the redeemed of the LORD shall return, and come with singing unto Zion; and everlasting joy shall be upon their head: they shall obtain gladness and joy; and sorrow and mourning shall flee away.

Isaiah 51:11

We are the redeemed of the Lord. We should not be moping and depressed, downtrodden and dreary. We have a right to be full of joy. We are the ones who should be putting on the garment of praise and the laughter and shouts of freedom. We should let our light shine and cast off sorrow and crying. We are on the winning side, the victor's side. He has won. No more fear, no more running, only joy, only peace.

"The Spirit of the Lord God is upon me; because the LORD hath anointed me to preach good tidings unto the meek; he hath sent me to bind up the brokenhearted, to proclaim liberty to the captives, and the opening of the prison to them that are bound; To proclaim the acceptable year of the LORD, and the day of vengeance of our God; to comfort all that mourn; To appoint unto them that mourn in Zion, to give unto them beauty for ashes, the oil of joy for mourning, the garment of praise for the spirit of heaviness; that they

might be called trees of righteousness, the planting of the LORD, that he might be glorified."

Isaiah 61:1-3

In Luke 4:21, Jesus spoke this passage and said, "This day is this scripture fulfilled in your ears." Jesus came to set us free. He came to preach the good news to us, to bind up the brokenhearted, to proclaim liberty to the captives. He came to do all these things for us. He came to heal our hearts but not only that. He also came to make us strong in Him that we might cast off that spirit of heaviness and put on the garment of praise. He has given us all that we need to be like Him, for He is in us. We have His Spirit. He's provided and given us His authority so that we, in turn, can go out and preach the gospel and set the captives free. He has passed the baton of life to us. All of these wondrous works glorify Him. He did great works, and greater works shall we do in His name because He has gone to the Father.

"David said moreover, The LORD that delivered me out of the paw of the lion, and out of the paw of the bear, he will deliver me out of the hand of this Philistine. And Saul said unto David, Go, and the LORD be with thee."

1 Samuel 17:37

Even in the physical we can look to our God to deliver and protect us. There are plenty of promises for that. We take them and stand on them. We believe and speak them, fully expecting that He is real and protection is ours. David discovered this truth. For him to say that the Lord delivered him means that David was looking to the Lord to help him. He wasn't counting on his own strength. He knew that he was no match for the bear and the lion by himself. We can trust in God for all things. When we get rid of the pride and humble ourselves under His mighty hand, He will lift us up. He will deliver. The uncircumcised Philistine was no match for God. Keep your eyes on God and His mighty ability. If we look at the problem, it grows big in our eyes. If we look to God, we will see His greatness.

"He delivereth me from mine enemies: yea, thou lifteth me up above those that rise up against me: thou hast delivered me from the violent man."

Psalm 18:48

Your enemies are God's enemies. Satan is our enemy, and he hates anyone that God loves, but he was no match for God. God sent Jesus. He lifted us up out of hell. We, in all rights, were destined for hell. But God, in His grace and mercy, delivered us and brought us up with Him to sit in heavenly places in Christ Jesus. We have been made joint heirs with Christ (Romans 8:17).

"I sought the LORD, and he heard me, and delivered me from all my fears."

Psalm 34:4

When we seek the Lord and draw near to Him, He draws near to us. He has already pursued you. He hears His children. And if you want to receive Jesus as your Lord, He hears your call. All that call upon the name of the Lord shall be saved (Romans 10:13). He delivers you from ALL your fears. Not one shall stay in your heart. You can have complete confidence as you trust in Him and His word. You are in a new family now that loves, provides, and delivers.

"For great is thy mercy toward me: and thou hast delivered my soul from the lowest hell."

Psalm 86:13

He does not save us out of obligation. He doesn't bring it up later and remind you of all the trouble you caused. He loves you, and His mercy is great toward you. He wanted to come to your rescue. He couldn't wait to ransom you, to forever adopt and care for you as His very own. God gave His Son. Jesus was willing to go and die. He went to the lowest depths of hell for you in your place. By the power of the Holy Spirit, He was raised from hell and from the dead. You have been raised with Christ. He has delivered your soul.

"He sent his word and healed them, and delivered them from their destructions."

Psalm 107:20

The Word that He sent was Jesus, and Jesus healed us. That is His nature: to help, to heal, and to save. He is the one who delivered. You may have noticed that this is all past tense. He sent, he healed, and he delivered. Jesus delivered us from our destructions. We were on our way to our destruction; this is where we were headed. He stopped it.

"For thou hast delivered my soul from death, mine eyes from tears, and my feet from falling."

Psalm 116:8

Those that do not receive his free gift of righteousness and redemption will inevitably go to hell; this is where we were all headed. He will not force us to choose Him. The Father is gracious and has given us a free will. We are the ones that must choose. His hope is that we choose Him, choose life, and choose Jesus. God is not willing that any should perish but that all should come to repentance (2 Peter 3:9). His heart is that all would be saved. But all will not be; some will choose Jesus, while others will hate Jesus.

"But thou hast in love to my soul delivered it from the pit of corruption: for thou has cast all my sins behind thy back."

Isaiah 38:17

Because He loved me, He was motivated to deliver me. He delivered my soul from the pit of corruption. I would have suffered in agony and terror were it not for my Savior and deliverer, for He has cast all my sins behind His back. He bore my grief and carried my sorrows. He was wounded for my transgressions and bruised for my iniquities. He took my load on His back. I was to carry it; it was mine. But He took it for me out of love.

"He delivereth and rescueth, and he worketh signs and wonders in heaven and in earth, who hath delivered Daniel from the power of the lions."

Daniel 6:27

The Lord is faithful to us. He is trustworthy and loyal, and we can put our utmost trust in Him. Heaven and earth will pass away, but His Word shall not pass away (Matthew 24:35). Even way back with Daniel and the lions' den, God was faithful; Daniel put his trust in God. He knew God would be with him. We must trust in God, in His power, to rescue us and deliver us. It is good to meditate on the miracles and wonders of God and to meditate on the works and miracles of Jesus in the gospels. We must imagine these wonderful things so that we can expect for signs and wonders to happen in our lives and through us. Jesus is the same today as He was yesterday and as He will always be.

"Then saith Jesus unto him, Get thee hence, Satan: for it is written, Thou shalt worship the Lord thy God, and him only shalt thou serve. Then the devil leaveth him, and, behold, angels came and ministered unto him."

Matthew 4:10–11

Jesus spoke to Satan. He spoke the Word. We cannot be passive or silent. The enemy will bring destruction if we are silent. Faith speaks. Jesus commanded him to leave; then He spoke the Word. If Jesus did this, we need to follow His example. This is the account of when Jesus fasted 40 days and 40 nights.

He was hungry, and the angels came to minister to Him. God met His need. Satan hates God's Word and doesn't want us to know its power and strength or its truth. We must get to know God's Word. We must meditate on it and know the truth of the Word deep in our hearts so in times of need, we are ready to draw our sword, which is the Word of God, and pierce the darkness with its power.

"And, behold, there arose a great tempest in the sea, insomuch that the ship was covered with the waves: but he was asleep. And his disciples came to him, and awoke him, saying, Lord, save us: we perish. And he saith unto them, Why are ye fearful, O ye of little faith? Then he arose, and rebuked the winds and the sea; and there was a great calm."

Matthew 8:24–26

Jesus was not ruled by fear; He refused fear. He knew where it came from and what damage it could do if he opened his heart to it. He was led by the Spirit of God, by the Word of God, and by the peace of God. He knew His authority. He knew God was with Him. He was not ruled by circumstances. This was a great tempest that arose in the sea, enough so that the ship was covered with waves. That is pretty extreme, and yet Jesus was asleep. The disciples feared and were coming to Him to instigate fear in Him as well, but He would not have it. You either have faith or fear; if you have a lot of faith, you will have little or no fear. If you have a lot of fear, you may have little faith. Will we give in to fear or faith? He arose and took charge, for they would not. He rebuked the winds and the sea in His authority, and in the end, there was a great calm.

"And when he was come to the other side into the country of the Gergesenes, there met him two possessed with devils, coming out of the tombs, exceeding fierce, so that no man might pass by that way…So the devils besought him, saying, If thou cast us out, suffer us to go away into the herd of swine.

"And he said unto them, Go. And when they were come out, they went into the herd of swine: and behold, the whole herd of swine ran violently down a steep place into the sea, and perished in the waters."

Matthew 8:28, 31–32

There is none that can stand up to the Lord of lords and the King of kings. Jesus is Lord, and He was not intimidated by any demon or any religious authority. Demons may have frightened the villagers away and showed themselves to be fierce, but they had to bow to Jesus. They were terrified of Him. They even asked if they could be allowed to go into the herd of pigs so that they could have a place to go. They need to have a body to be able to roam on this earth. He said, "Go," and they did. The whole herd of pigs ran violently down a steep hill into the sea and drowned in the water.

We must keep our eyes on the one who is able to deliver, not the demons who deceive and have no authority. We stand behind the name, not in our own name. They are afraid of the name and His Word. But they also know when a believer does not really know their authority in Christ.

"As they went out, behold, they brought to him a dumb man possessed with a devil. And when the devil was cast out, the dumb spake: and the multitude marveled, saying, It was never so seen in Israel."

Matthew 9:32–33

They brought to Jesus a man who was dumb and couldn't speak, for he was possessed with a demon that apparently caused the man not to speak. Jesus knew all things. He knew it was a demon. It doesn't say how long this man was possessed, but when Jesus cast the demon out, the man was able to speak. There was a multitude or a throng of people that wondered and marveled, saying, "They had never seen this in Israel."

"Then was brought unto him one possessed with a devil, blind, and dumb: and he healed him, insomuch that the blind and dumb both spake and saw."

Matthew 12:22

This demon had caused the man to be blind and not to speak. There are times when demons attack the body in different ways, but we should never be afraid or be in terror of any demons, for they have been stripped and defeated. They have no power over us. Jesus has all power and has defeated the kingdom of darkness. Jesus healed this man, and he was free to see and free to speak. Praise God!

"And there was in their synagogue a man with an unclean spirit; and he cried out, saying, Let us alone; what have we to do with thee, thou Jesus of Nazareth? art thou come to destroy us? I know thee who thou art, Holy One of God. And Jesus rebuked him, saying, Hold thy peace, and come out of him. And when the unclean spirit had torn him, and cried with a loud voice, he came out of him."

Mark 1:23–26

This man was even in their synagogue, among them, with an unclean spirit. Maybe even several demons for they said, "Let us alone." They knew who He was—the holy one of God. We don't have to have conversations with demons, for they lie. Jesus told it to hold its peace, to be quiet. He said simply said, "Come out of him."

Amplified says, "And the unclean spirit throwing the man into convulsions, and screeching with a loud voice, came out of him." The demon may have thrown a fit after Jesus commanded him to leave, but he did leave.

"And Jesus answering saith unto them, Have faith in God. For verily I say unto you, That whosoever shall say unto this mountain, Be thou removed, and be thou cast into the sea; and shall not doubt in his heart, but shall believe that those things which he saith shall come to pass; he shall have whatsoever he saith. Therefore I say unto you, What things soever ye desire, when ye pray, believe that ye receive them, and ye shall have them."

Mark 11:22–24

Jesus said, "Have faith in God." The Amplified explains this phrase as "Have faith in God constantly." To have faith in God is to trust Him, to believe Him and what He says. Sometimes we fail because we are looking to ourselves. We think that we are not strong enough to believe or that we are unable to believe, but it is easy to believe that God can do anything. It is not supposed to be a struggle. Just decide to believe Him. Whosoever shall say to this mountain—what is your mountain? Throughout our lives, there will be many mountains for as long as we are in this world. You alone must speak to your mountain. Sometimes another believer can come alongside of you and pray for you, but you might as well learn to speak to the mountain as God intended you to.

Death and life are in the power of the tongue. This is how the kingdom of God operates. In the beginning, God spoke. Speak death to the mountain and life to your future. Envision it. Picture it in your heart. Remember, it's not according to your feelings.

"And he said unto them, Go ye into all the world, and preach the gospel to every creature. He that believeth and is baptized shall be saved; but he that believeth not shall be damned. And these signs shall follow them that believe; In my name shall they cast out devils; they shall speak with new tongues; They shall take up serpents; and if they drink any deadly thing, it shall not hurt them; they shall lay hands on the sick, and they shall recover. So then after the Lord had spoken unto them, he was received up into heaven, and sat on the right hand of God. And they went forth, and preached every where, the Lord working with them, and confirming the word with signs following. Amen."

Mark 16:15–20

These are some of the last instructions from Jesus to the disciples. In this instruction, the first word he uses is "Go." This is a verb, an action word. He is telling us what to do. We are the ones who will be doing it. He told us to go into all the world, to go and preach the gospel to everyone. The power of God is in the gospel (Romans 1:16). As you preach the gospel, signs will follow. The key is to believe. These signs will follow those that believe. We will be doing these works not in our own power but in the name of Jesus. These are not ordinary, everyday signs in the world. Most people don't go around casting out demons and speaking in new tongues. This is not the Old Testament—this is New Testament living. And this was spoken after Jesus was raised from the dead. He spoke this just before He went to heaven to be with the Father. After He had spoken to them, He went to sit at the right hand of God. So they obeyed and preached everywhere. The Lord was in heaven, yes, but His Spirit was also living in them and working with them. They were not alone; He promised He would never leave them (Hebrews 13:5). He did as He promised, and He confirmed His word with signs.

"But Jesus beheld them, and said unto them, With men this is impossible; but with God all things are possible."

Matthew 19:26

Men are the creation from God. They are not God. Without His Spirit, we are nothing. With His Spirit, we have everything. We have His ability. Men, in themselves, are limited. They cannot accomplish what the almighty God can accomplish. Consider His majestic power. He is the creator of the crackling thunder and lightning. He made the breaking waves and the roar of the ocean deep. The clouds above all the earth were formed by Him alone, and He caused the rain to pour from the heavens. God alone made the lions that roam free and the whales of the blue sea that frolic full of power. Who can tell the Almighty what to do? With God, all things are possible!

"And he said unto them, I beheld Satan as lightning fall from heaven. Behold, I give unto you power to tread on serpents and scorpions, and over all the power of the enemy: and nothing shall by any means hurt you."

Luke 10:18–19

Jesus is the "I am." He was there when Satan fell as lightning from heaven. He saw Satan stripped of his power and authority, not to mention all of his beauty. To all means you are no longer in that place you were in. He fell because of pride. He was humbled by God, for he would not humble himself.

Jesus is the one with all authority. When He died on the cross, descended into hell, and rose again on the third day, He conquered

Satan. He took the keys of hell and death and gave us authority. We have the power to tread on serpents and scorpions and over all the power of the enemy, and nothing shall by any means hurt you.

You must use your faith and believe this in order to enjoy its benefits. His will is that you are protected. He thought of everything.

"For God so loved the world, that he gave his only begotten Son, that whosoever believeth in him should not perish, but have everlasting life."

John 3:16

God SO loved the world. There is no one that can ever say, "God doesn't love me." God's Word is truth and does not lie. This scripture states that He so loved the world. If you are on the earth today, that includes you. He proved His love by giving of His only Son. The scripture continues to say, "Whosoever." That also includes you, for each person, each human being, is a whosoever.

"Jesus answered and said unto her, Whosoever drinketh of this water shall thirst again: But whosoever drinketh of the water that I shall give him shall never thirst; but the water that I shall give him shall be in him a well of water springing up into everlasting life."

John 4:13–14

This can be spoken to any one of us. He is offering us a drink of the water that He gives us. It is not the same as the water we know, although you can look at the water that we are used to drinking as a parallel. We need water tolive. We must have it to survive. But the issue with the physical water is that it needs to be replenished. Our thirst is quenched until we get thirsty again. With His Spirit living in us, we drink from the living waters. It is possible to be full, and stay full, as we let the Word of God dwell richly in us.

"I am the living bread which came down from heaven: if any man eat of this bread, he shall live for ever: and the bread that I will give is my flesh, which I will give for the life of the world."

John 6:51

Jesus came down from heaven. He calls Himself the living bread, the Word. We are to eat this bread. The fleshly body needs bread to eat each day to sustain life. We also need to eat of His Word every day to sustain us, to grow, and to be nourished and strengthened. As we accept Jesus and eat of Him, we shall live forever. Through His giving of His body, His life, the whole world is now able to have life because of Him. Without partaking of Him continually, you will have no life.

"It is the spirit that quickeneth; the flesh profiteth nothing: the words that I speak unto you, they are spirit, and they are life."

John 6:63

The Spirit brings life, and His words are spirit, for they come from Him. Everything that comes from Him is life. When His spirit brings life to our spirit, it permeates through all of our being. His words are life to all of our flesh. They bring peace and life to our minds. The world puts great stock in having a perfect and beautiful outside body, but many do nothing on the inside. The kingdom of God starts from the inside out.

"The thief cometh not, but for to steal, and to kill, and to destroy; I am come that they might have life, and that they might have it more abundantly."

John 10:10

Why should we let Satan, who is the thief, steal from our lives any longer? As we dwell on the past and speak of the past, we are only helping him to dig our own grave. Why should we help him? He is the enemy, and he is defeated. Jesus came that we might have life and that we might have it more abundantly. The ones that come and receive and take it will be the ones who receive it.

"But ye shall receive power, after that the Holy Ghost is come upon you: and ye shall be witnesses unto me both in Jerusalem, and in all Judaea, and in Samaria, and unto the uttermost part of the earth."

Acts 1:8

Jesus didn't want to leave us alone. You can read more about the Holy Spirit in John 14. He is meant to be our helper and comforter, our advocate, and our teacher. He would not have given us the gift of the Holy Spirit unless we needed Him. With Him, we have the power of God to be witnesses throughout the earth. The Holy Spirit also gives us boldness and power to have a more victorious Christian life. The Holy Ghost is a gift, and as you invite Him, He shall come upon you and you shall receive power from on high.

"And when the day of Pentecost was fully come, they were all with one accord in one place. And suddenly there came a sound from heaven as of a rushing mighty wind, and it filled all the house where they were sitting. And there appeared unto them cloven tongues like as of fire, and it sat upon each of them. And they were all filled with the Holy Ghost, and began to speak with other tongues, as the Spirit gave them utterance."

Acts 2:1–4

The disciples were all in unity, waiting. What was it like to hear this sound of a rushing mighty wind from heaven? Their hair and clothes must have been blowing as they sat waiting for this adventure. What an exciting experience God gave them. They were each amazed as they saw the lights of fire resting upon each of them. Every one of them were filled; Acts 1:15 says that there were 120 of them. When we receive the Holy Spirit, we have His power in us—the supernatural power of God. We were not meant to be ordinary. If the power of God that created the universe and raised Christ from the dead lives in you, how can you see yourself as only ordinary? We are His vessels; He moves through us, heals through us, and delivers through us. Tongues are a blessing that comes from God above. And God only gives good gifts.

"I am the door; by me if any man enter in, he shall be saved, and shall go in and out, and find pasture."

John 10:9

Always remember that Jesus is the door. He is the way, the truth, and the life. No man comes to the Father but by Him. He did the work; we receive the grace. It is not by our works, but by His works, His performance. Only He can save, and only He can give the rest that we need. Only He can provide the sweet freedom that we so desperately needed. All that is required is that we open the door and walk in. He did the work, and now He is waiting for you to respond. Walk and enter in the door of life, which is Jesus Christ, today.

Meditations 2 – I Am Blessed

The word "blessed" shows up 205 times in the Old Testament, along with the word "blessing," which shows up 60 times. We have been taught that God is out to strike us and bring us down. This is a lie. When we look up the word "cursed," we see it only 64 times in the Old Testament and "cursing" only 10 times. This should be an eye opener to us.

"And God blessed them, saying, Be fruitful, and multiply, and fill the waters in the seas, and let fowl multiply in the earth."

Genesis 1:22

The first thing that God did was bless. It's as if He said, "Now you go and be a blessing." To be fruitful is to be a blessing; to multiply is all about abundance.

So we are talking about an abundance of blessings. Everything that God created was meant to be fruitful and to multiply, from Adam and Eve and their kind on to all the animals, the fish, and their kind. The earth was not meant tobe sparse but full and flourishing, rich and lush. This is God's way.

"And he blessed him, and said, Blessed be Abram of the most high God, possessor of heaven and earth:"

Genesis 14:19

Abram was blessed, and not by just anyone but by the most high God, possessor of heaven and earth. It is God who owns the earth and the heavens. He made and created it and everything in it. They belong to Him. When you think about it, we also belong to Him. It is man that strayed away, not God. In man's rebellion, many think they own their own life. In God's mercy, He has given man a free will, but He wants man to choose life, choose Him. Psalm 115:15–16 says, "Ye are blessed of the LORD who made heaven and earth. The heaven, even the heavens, are the LORD's: but the earth hath he given to the children of men." He not only gave us a free will but decided to give us the earth to have dominion over it; you can read this in Genesis 1.

"And he said, I am Abraham's servant. And the LORD hath blessed my master greatly; and he is become great: and he hath given him flocks, and herds, and silver, and gold, and menservants, and maidservants, and camels, and asses.

Genesis 24:34–35

Abram's name originally meant "exalted father." Later God changed it to Abraham, which means "father of a multitude." Why was he so blessed? Genesis 15:6 says that Abram believed God, and it was counted to him for righteousness. He trusted God and took Him at His word. God told him that he would be the father of many nations. Abram was an old man, and his wife was barren, but he believed God. He obeyed God. Obedience and trust bring blessings. God loves when we trust Him. Isaiah 1:19 states: "If ye be willing and obedient, ye shall eat the good of the land." As we trust God and believe that He is who He says He is, we will be blessed in every area of our lives. Blessings will overtake us, and favor will be upon us and our children and our children's children. It will happen!

"So the LORD *blessed the latter end of Job more than his beginning: for he had fourteen thousand sheep, and six thousand camels, and a thousand yoke of oxen, and a thousand she asses. He had also seven sons and three daughters."*

Job 42:12–13

God is a God of restoration. It is Satan who steals and destroys, according to John 10:10. It is God who builds and replenishes, who gives life, also according to John 10:10. If you read the book of Job carefully, you will see that it was Satan who came in and stole and destroyed all that Job had. And in the very end, it wasGod who came in and blessed all that was stolen. He restored more than Job had in the beginning. Joel 2:25 speaks of how God restores all the years that the locust has eaten. Isaiah 61:7 reminds us that he will restore a double portion. If you have experienced your life being ripped from you, it would do you well to take these scriptures and hold on tight to them. Dare to believe them and see them come to pass in your life till every last thing that was stolen is replaced. Jesus has paid for this to happen.

"But his delight is in the law of the LORD; *and in his law doth he meditate day and night. And he shall be like a tree planted by the rivers of water, that bringeth forth his fruit in his season; his leaf also shall not wither; and whatsoever he doeth shall prosper."*

Psalm 1:2–3

His Word was meant to be delighted in. His Word can give us joy, and we can actually come to the point where we can fall in love with His Word, for it is alive. John 1:14 says, "And the Word was made flesh, and dwelt among us, (and we beheld his glory, the glory as of the only begotten of the Father,) full of grace and truth." I have experienced loving the Word of God. I didn't used to, to be honest. I made the decision to think on and meditate on the Scriptures. I made myself refuse to think onmy problems. Everyone has problems, but I decided to fix my mind on His Word throughout the day. It took a few months to get in the habit, but it began to change me from the inside out. It brought peace to my soul. It began to speak to me; I began to understand it. The Holy Spirit helped me and taught me in this. I became more grateful and less negative. But each day I had to choose this way. Things began to change for the better in every area of my life. Favor and blessings followed me.

"The LORD is my shepherd, I shall not want."

Psalm 23:1

If you have a shepherd, this means that you are a follower. It means someone else is sitting in the driver's seat. It also means He will provide for you. You will not be in any need or have any lack for anything. For what does a shepherd do? He protects and feeds. He provides for his sheep. He leads them out of harm's way. All the sheep does is feed and rest and enjoy the benefits of the shepherd. God loves to provide for His sheep, and He can do a much better job than you or I can. We can lead, but our lives will be greatly limited. If He leads, our lives' potential will be unlimited. So the end result will be: I shall not want for anything, physically or spiritually.

"O taste and see that the LORD is good: blessed is the man that trusteth in him. O fear the LORD, ye his saints: for there is no want to them that fear him. The young lions do lack and suffer hunger: but they that seek the LORD shall not want any good thing."

Psalm 34:8–10

Those who trust Him will also love His Word. You will trust His word and take Him at His word. His word is sweeter than honey; Psalm 119:103 says, "How sweet are thy words unto my taste! yea, sweeter than honey to my mouth!"

To fear the Lord is to revere Him. The lion may be hungry, may lack, but we who seek God, who revere Him and trust Him, will not lack any good thing. We will not need anything; He will take care of us and provide for us. We are blessed.

"I have been young, and now am old; yet have I not seen the righteous forsaken, nor his seed begging bread. He is ever merciful, and lendeth; and his seed is blessed."

Psalm 37:25–26

These are the words of King David. He is speaking of his whole life, from youth to being elderly. Throughout his life, he never saw the righteous forsaken, meaning they were never left. David lived a long life, and God always met his needs. God blessed him so that he was on the other end of the beggar. He was the lender, and his seed, or his children, were blessed. They probably saw the example of their parents and became lenders and blessed as well. Children learn what they live. David had a heart after God, and so did his son Solomon.

"For with thee is the fountain of life:"

Psalm 36:9

We were made to be dependent creatures. As humans, we were made to drink and get thirsty on a regular basis. If we don't drink, we die. What makes us think it is any different spiritually? He is the fountain of life. The problem is that most people don't know there is such a fountain. We think we can make it on our own— we are the source of our lives. Our Father wants to be the source of our lives. Within Him is the fountain. Only He can truly fill us and satisfy our longing hearts. Imagine being fully loved, blessed, and satisfied every single day.

I believe it is possible, even on this earth. As we practice His presence and learn to come to Him to receive of His fullness through His Word and His Spirit, we shall walk in the blessing we were intended to walk in. Verse 8 states, "They shall be abundantly satisfied with the fatness of thy house; and thou shalt make them drink of the river of thy pleasures.

"Blessed is the man that maketh the LORD his trust."
Psalm 40:4

He is a smart man that trusts God. And reading this verse tells us we have to do it. We have to make the Lord our trust. When we do this, we are blessed because He will prove that His Word can provide. Blessings will be the result of trusting.

"Blessed is he that considereth the poor: the LORD will deliver him in time of trouble. The LORD will preserve him and keep him alive; and he shall be blessed upon the earth: and thou wilt not deliver him unto the will of his enemies."
Psalm 41:1–2

To consider is to think about, to understand, and to care about what the Lord cares about. When we take care of what is dear to Him, He will take care of what is dear to us. Luke 6:38 says, "Give, and it shall be given unto you; good measure, pressed down, and shaken together, shall men give into your bosom." But who is the one who puts it on men's hearts to give? If you deliver someone out of trouble, God will deliver you. Those who are blessed on the earth are the ones who are blessing others. They can't help it; it comes from the overflow of the good Father.

"Blessed be the LORD, who daily loadeth us with benefits, even the God of our salvation."

Psalm 68:19

This word "loadeth" in Hebrew actually means to impose a burden on. He wants to bless you; His will is to load you with benefits and blessings. We should bless Him and thank Him, not whine and complain. In Psalm 23, it speaks of how "he anoints my head with oil, my cup runneth over." The Father is not thinking about the waste that spills over. He cares more that you realize. He cares more that you get to the point where you know that abundance belongs to you. God will never run out of blessings— that is impossible. He is the God of your salvation. He has saved you from death and poverty.

"Blessed are they that dwell in thy house: they will still be praising thee. Selah. Blessed is the man whose strength is in thee; in whose heart are the ways of them. Who passing through the valley of Baca make it a well; the rain also filleth the pools. They go from strength to strength, every one of them in Zion appeared before God."

Psalm 84:4-7

Those who are keeping themselves God centered and Jesus centered by abiding in Him—those who live by His Word, putting it first above circumstances and feelings—will find their strength in Him. They that love to worship and be in His presence and who keep fellowship with him—who are at home in His presence and in His Word—will find their strength in Him and nowhere else. As they are connected with Him, He infuses His love, power, and ability to and through them.

Baca is the Hebrew word for weeping or mourning, even complaining. But as I read it and see that the people have their strength in the Lord, they only pass by it. They do not stay. They even make it a well. To have His strength is to wait on Him, to be still and be refreshed so that you are full. Strength to strength, glory to glory. We will not be complainers, for we do not need to be!

"For the LORD God is a sun and shield: the LORD will give grace and glory: no good thing will he withhold from them that walk uprightly."

Psalm 84:11

Our sun is blindingly bright, offering warmth and light to everyone on Earth. It was created by God, the one whom light stems from. He is the source of all light and power and energy. He is our shield. The ones that walk uprightly will be the ones that benefit from Him the most, the ones who know Him. We are now in the new covenant through the cross of Jesus. Through Jesus, grace and glory have been given freely. Jesus has provided all by His obedience, and He will withhold no good thing from His children, but we must receive it by faith through grace.

"The righteous shall flourish like the palm tree: he shall grow like a cedar in Lebanon. Those that be planted in the house of the LORD shall flourish in the courts of our God. They shall still bring forth fruit in old age; they shall be fat and flourishing; to shew that the LORD is upright: he is my rock, and there is no unrighteousness in him."

Psalm 92:12–14

The righteous run on different energy than the rest of the world. We have food that they do not know of and have never tasted. We just keep flourishing because of the Spirit and His Word and His presence. When a sponge is dry, it has to wait until it is soaked and wet to be full again. It is possible to never run dry but to have His rivers of living water flowing constantly, refreshing ourselves and everyone we come into contact with. We are the righteous in Christ Jesus. The cedars in Lebanon are tall, and you will see that some spread out horizontally. Plant yourself in the presence of the Lord often. When we worship, we get back into balance in our emotions. We get centered, receiving His precious peace. It doesn't matter how old we are or where we are in our walk; we can have fruit and an abundant life that is flourishing so that people can see it on our faces. This is a representation of the Lord—you are showing that He is upright.

"Blessed is the man whom thou chasteneth, O LORD, and teachest him out of thy law; that thou mayest give him rest from the days of adversity…"
Psalm 94:12–13

When you know that your Father loves you for who you are, you can handle his correction. He loves you so much that He is watching out for and thinking of your future, just like a good father here on the earth, who raises his son right and shows him the way to success. He cares about his son's future. He doesn't want to see him fail or sweating the rest of his life. A good father desires to see his child blessed, happy, healthy, and leading a very productive life.

"Who redeemeth thy life from destruction; who crowneth thee with lovingkindness and tender mercies; who satisfieth thy mouth with good things; so that thy youth is renewed like the eagle's."
Psalm 103:4–5

God is the one who redeems your life from destruction. He is the one who crowns you with lovingkindness and tender mercies. He satisfies your mouth with good things so that your youth is renewed like the eagle's. If you think about it, this is exactly what Jesus did on the cross for you. He provided a way forblessing, an avenue for wholeness. The good things in your mouth can be physical and spiritual. He created good food that is good for our bodies, but He also gave us His Word, as it says in Proverbs 4:20–23. It is the Scriptures that bring life to all that find them and healing to all of their flesh.

"Praise ye the LORD. *Blessed is the man that feareth the* LORD, *that delighteth greatly in his commandments. His seed shall be mighty upon the earth: the generation of the upright shall be blessed. Wealth and riches shall be in his house: and his righteousness endureth forever."*

Psalm 112:1–3

Blessed is the man that doesn't merely delight in His commandments but who also greatly delights in them. Be honest with yourself, and think about what you take great delight in. Consider what that is and how it makes you feel. He wants us to feel that way about His Word.

For the seed to be mighty on the earth means that the parent has already been mighty first; the child follows suit. His generation will be blessed. Wealth and riches will be in the house of the righteous, and he will leave a legacy. His righteousness will endure forever— not because of us but because it is the righteousness of Jesus. It never ends but goes on forever.

"For every beast of the forest is mine, and the cattle upon a thousand hills."

Psalm 50:10

He who creates something is the owner of it, and he can do what he wants with his creation. God chooses to exercise His lovingkindness on His creation. Imagine every beast of the world—hippos, bears, eagles, tigers, owls. Think of all the many kinds of species of animals. He has such an imagination. They are all His, and He created all of the different habitats they live in. Each type of food for them is also unique. He made them and everything they need to sustain them. He didn't miss a thing. To say the cattle upon a thousand hills are His is to say all animals are His.

"He will bless them that fear the LORD, both small and great. The LORD shall increase you more and more, you and your children. Ye are blessed of the LORD which made heaven and earth. The heaven, even the heavens, are the LORD's: but the earth hath he given to the children of men."

Psalm 115:13–16

The proud do not fear the Lord, for they do not need Him. They think they only need themselves; they are not humble. But those that are humble fear the Lord, and for this, they are blessed. You can be great and still be humble and fear the Lord. Look at David, for example. He was great, but he feared the Lord. What will happen to you when you do this is what happened to David. God will increase you more and more and your children as well. Can you picture yourself being blessed by the creator who made heaven and earth?

And that's not all. The heavens are His, but He even went so far as to give the earth to the children of men. This goes along with Genesis 1, in which He said He gave man dominion over the earth.

"O give thanks unto the LORD; for he is good: because his mercy endureth forever."

Psalm 119:1

We should give God thanks for all He has done and for His goodness. Too often we are focused on the problems of this world. And when the new day comes, well, we are so used to thinking on problems that if we don't have any, we will create new ones. It becomes, in a twisted way, a comfort zone. God's peace should be our only comfort zone.

"Blessed is every one that feareth the LORD; that walketh in his ways. For thou shall eat the labor of thy hands: happy shalt thou be, and it shall be well with thee."

Psalm 128:1–2

Again we see another scripture about fearing the Lord. These are the blessed ones, the ones who fear Him. When one fears the Lord, he is humbling himself and surrendering to God as higher than all—wiser and all powerful. When you are in total charge of your own life, you will not look to God or anyone else for guidance. When you look to Him, you are much better off, for He is the wisest of all and can see ahead, where we cannot. You will walk in His ways because you trust in Him. As you submit to Him, He will give you wisdom so that you can do good labor and then eat the fruit of that labor. And happy shall you be, and all shall be well with you.

"For he hath strengthened the bars of thy gates; he hath blessed thy children within thee. He maketh peace in thy borders, and filleth thee with the finest of the wheat. He sendeth forth his commandment upon the earth: his word runneth very swiftly."

Psalm 147:13–15

He has strengthened the bars of your gates because he is your defender, your protector. All that you have is blessed; rest upon this truth. Your children in the womb are blessed, and so expect them to be formed by His hands as whole and healthy. He is your provider, not just filling your house with wheat but the finest of wheat. His word is alive and powerful, sharp and quick. He sent His word,which is Jesus; Jesus and the Word are one. As He sends forth His Word, it does not return void or empty. It is truth, and it does what it has set out to do. His Word runs very swiftly; trust it.

"Now therefore hearken unto me, O ye children: for blessed are they that keep my ways. Hear instruction, and be wise, refuse it not. Blessed is the man that heareth me, watching daily at my gates, waiting at the posts of my doors. For whoso findeth me findeth life, and shall obtain favour of the LORD."

Proverbs 8:32–35

It is a good thing to remain humble and teachable. Avoid pride, for it will prevent your ability to be taught and to learn from him. His word will make you wise, so do not refuse it.

Listen and watch daily for His wisdom. Be swift to listen and slow to speak. Wait and be patient, not anxious and hasty. When a person finds it, that means he has been looking. And as you seek it, you will find life. At the same time you will get favor from the Lord. He is so pleased when His children trust Him.

"He becometh poor that dealeth with a slack hand: but the hand of the diligent maketh rich. He that gathereth in summer is a wise son: but he that sleepeth in harvest is a son that causeth shame. Blessings are upon the head of the just: but violence covereth the mouth of the wicked. The memory of the just is blessed..."

Proverbs 10:4–7

To be slack means to be lazy. So if you are slow and lazy in giving, you will become poor. This makes no sense to most people, but when you understand the kingdom's ways, you will know that to give is to plant seeds, which means that they will multiply and give you a harvest. Be diligent to plant seed; doing it with a right and joyful heart will increase you. It will make you rich. God will bless the work of your hands. Can you imagine sleeping in the middle of a harvest? Here you plant a garden, water it, and tend for the weeds, and when the time comes to harvest, you close your door and just go to sleep. Blessings are on your head if you are His child.

All that is about you is blessed, even the memory of you, even your words and the end result of what your words produce. Not so with the evil. You know a tree by its fruit, and out of the evil come bad words and bad fruit. Even the memory of them gives a sad and regretful taste to the one who remembers them. You can choose to be a drain on people or a fountain that will bless. It is your choice.

"He that hath a bountiful eye shall be blessed; for he giveth of his bread to the poor."

Proverbs 22:9

Again, here is an example of a giver, a bountiful sower. Even his thoughts are not stingy and skimpy. Even his eye sees things through a giver's eye. He is always thinking, *What can I do for them? How can I help?* He considers the poor. He doesn't ignore and pass them. He stops to look at them. How many times do we pull up to a stoplight where there is a homeless person and we turn the other way and pretend they will go away. We try to make them disappear. Yes, we have to use wisdom, but in doing so, we don't have to ignore them. The one with the bountiful eye gives bread to the poor.

"She openeth her mouth with wisdom; and in her tongue is the law of kindness. She looketh well to the ways of her household, and eateth not the bread of idleness. Her children arise up, and call her blessed; her husband also, and he praiseth her."

Proverbs 31:26–28

Let us look deeper. Out of the abundance of the heart the mouth speaks. This truly stems from the thoughts she thinks and dwells on. Remember, as a man thinks in his heart, so is he. She, therefore, thought and saw kindness, wisdom, and blessing to her family; she thought of being busy, to do well for them.

We can choose to be what we want. We can choose to be a victim. But if we do, we'll think like a victim and picture ourselves that way. We'll think that everyone is out to get us. You will attract what you think, but you can change that and think on the good instead. See yourself as a blessing, and speak blessings over yourself. Think something like, *I am a blessing to my family. I lean on the strength and wisdom of the Lord to help me every day. I follow His lead and not my own.* Your children will bless and praise you, not curse you. Your husband will praise you in the gates. He will trust you because you give him reason to trust you.

"Then shall he give the rain of thy seed, that thou shalt sow the ground withal; and bread of increase of the earth, and it shall be fat and plenteous: in that day shall thy cattle feed in large pastures."

Isaiah 30:2

He is our God and our source for all things. He gives us seed, and He gives us rain to water the seed. His way is not only to supply our needs but to supply with an abundant supply. An earthly father would give a good inheritance to His children but may always hope for more to leave—the more the better. God is so capable of supplying richly and continually with love. The real problem lies in us not receiving or believing. We don't think He wants to do these things for us. Notice the very last phrase: "in large pastures." That is our Father in heaven. According to your faith, be it done unto you, my friend.

"But the liberal deviseth liberal things; and by liberal things shall he stand."

Isaiah 32:8

From the Message:

"But generous people plan to do what is generous. And they stand firm in their generosity."

To devise is to plan. There are some who enjoy devising evil and trickery. There are others who devise with thoughts of greed and consuming goods. They think on the next thing that they want to buy or collect. How different is it to think on and plan and devise ways of giving, as well as people to bless, and to imagine and create projects that will benefit others in your city, in your church, in your state, in your country, or in other countries around the world. His Spirit and that same generous spirit live in you if you know Jesus.

"And my people shall dwell in a peaceable habitation, and in sure dwellings, and in quiet resting places;"

Isaiah 32:18

Speak this one over your household and over your family. With Christ living in you, you have peace with God. You have peace living inside of you. This is a peace from heaven, one that passes all understanding. In your circumstances, there may be turmoil even all around, but it is possible for you, even through the turmoil, to be at peace and to not be moved. In the world, you will have tribulation, but be of good cheer, Jesus said, "I have overcome the world." He will keep you and sustain you in the eye of the storm.

"Look unto Abraham your father, and unto Sarah that bare you: for I called him alone, and blessed him, and increased him."

Isaiah 51:2

God is speaking to those who follow after righteousness. You can read the verse that comes before and see it for yourself. He says to look at Abraham, to think on his life. Remember how God blessed him. You can read about him in Genesis 12. God told him that He would make of him a great nation, that He would make his name great, and that he would be a blessing. God said He would bless them that bless him and curse them that curse him. This blessing all came from God the good father. God is the one who increased him, for that, remember, is God's way.

"Blessed is the man that trusteth in the LORD, and whose hope the LORD is. For he shall be as a tree planted by the waters, and that spreadeth out her roots by the river, and shall not see when heat cometh, but her leaf shall be green; and shall not be careful in the year of drought, neither shall cease from yielding fruit."

Jeremiah 17:7–8

My help in is the Lord, not in man. My hope is in the Lord and not in anything or anyone else. I shall be blessed because I trust in Him. I am as a tree planted by the waters, very strong and secure. By trusting in Him, I will be sustained. It is by my trust in His Word that I will grow and my leaf shall always be green.

I will not see when heat comes, because I won't be looking for it. I shall be keeping my eyes on the Lord. I will not be leading my life according to circumstances nor letting feelings guide my every step. It is possible to always be the same calm and peaceful person, never worried about the unpredictable weather or any threatening drought. It is possible to live with a continual harvest of fruit. Do not follow the world's way. It is by following God's kingdom principles that this is all possible.

"Bring ye all the tithes into the storehouse, that there may be meat in mine house, and prove me now herewith, saith the LORD of hosts, if I will not open you the windows of heaven, and pour you out a blessing, that there shall not be room enough to receive it. And I will rebuke the devourer for your sakes, and he shall not destroy the fruits of your ground; neither shall your vine cast her fruit before the time in the field, saith the LORD of hosts. And all nations shall call you blessed: for you shall be a delightsome land, saith the LORD of hosts."

Malachi 3:10–12

The word "all" does not mean that God is demanding every cent we have in a selfish way; His heart is to give and hold nothing back. He gives all of His blessing. He wants us to have the same heart—a giving attitude. You cannot out give God. Picture the windows of heaven opening out onto you, pouring out more than you need. Not only does He bless you back but He rebukes the devourer for your sake. The devourer will not destroy the fruit of your ground, and your harvest will come right on time. You will be so blessed that all the nations will see it, and they shall call you blessed. The Lord of hosts is the one who has spoken all of this. If He declares it, it shall be so.

Lastly, He states that you shall be a delightsome land! You are truly blessed. To give to the Lord is more for your good than anything else.

(Speaking of Abraham) "That in blessing I will bless thee, and in multiplying I will multiply thy seed as the stars of the heaven, and as the sand which is upon the sea shore; and thy seed shall possess the gate of his enemies; And in thy seed shall all the nations of the earth be blessed; because thou hast obeyed my voice."

Genesis 22:17–18

Our Father God gives a parallel using the stars and the grains of sand to explain just how much He will bless and multiply the seed of Abraham. Can you count the stars? Can anyone count the sand? The next phrase, I believe, is prophetic, speaking of Jesus and His finished work, the defeat of the enemy. He is the one who holds the keys of death and hell. "Thy seed shall possess the gate of his enemies." It is because of Jesus that we are blessed and included in Abraham's blessing. Galatians 3:29 tells us, "And if ye be Christ's, then are ye Abraham's seed, and heirs according to the promise."

"Then Isaac sowed in that land, and received in the same year an hundredfold: and the LORD blessed him. And the man waxed great, and went forward, and grew until he became very great: For he had possession of flocks, and possession of herds, and great store of servants: and the Philistines envied him."

Genesis 26:12–14

This is a perfect picture of how I believe a child of God could and should be living; it displays God's best. And he waxed great; he went forward, not backward. He grew and kept growing until he became very great. We are to prosper so much that we can't help but be the envy of the world around us. We should be the ones to loan and not borrow. The very first words in this passage are "Then Isaac sowed in that land." We are meant to be sowers and reapers, givers and blessers.

"And it shall come to pass, if thou shalt hearken diligently unto the voice of the LORD thy God, to observe and to do all his commandments which I command thee this day, that the LORD thy God will set thee on high above all nations of the earth: And all these blessings shall come on thee, and overtake thee, if thou shalt hearken unto the voice of the LORD thy God. Blessed shalt thou be in the city, and blessed shalt thou be in the field. Blessed shall be the fruit of thy body, and the fruit of thy ground, and the fruit of thy cattle, the increase of thy kine, and the flocks of thy sheep. Blessed shall be thy basket and thy store. Blessed shalt thou be when thou comest in, and blessed shalt thou be when thou goest out. The LORD shall cause thine enemies that rise up against thee to be smitten before thy face:they shall come out against thee one way, and flee before thee seven ways. The LORD shall command the blessing upon thee in thy storehouses, and in all that thou settest thine hand unto; and he shall bless thee in the land which the LORD thy God giveth thee."

Deuteronomy 28:1–8

In the Old Testament, in order to receive the blessings of God, you needed to be willing and obedient. In the New Testament, we receive these blessings by faith in Christ Jesus (Gal. 3:13–14). Verse 29 of this same chapter says, "And if ye be Christ's, then are ye Abraham's seed, and heirs according to the promise." Jesus did all the work on the cross and provided all that we would ever need. Healing is a gift. Provision is a gift. Peace with God is a gift. The blessings of God are gifts; we cannot buy them or earn them. They are free from God through Jesus because He loves us greatly. Receive these blessings. You are blessed in every area of your life, from your property, to your animals and gardens, to your family and your bank accounts. Speak these blessings over yourself often and see them operating in your life. See the enemy fleeing seven ways away from you. The favor of God is all around you, so what or whom shall we fear? We belong to the winning side.

"I call heaven and earth to record this day against you, that I have set before you life and death, blessing and cursing: therefore choose life, that both thou and thy seed may live:"

Deuteronomy 30:19

God asks us to choose. We are the ones who have the freedom to choose; He cannot make us. He gave us a free will. No one is twisting your arm. No one can make you happy but you. God has already given His Son, and Jesus has already defeated Satan.

John 10:10 says, "I am come that they might have life, and that they might have it more abundantly." Not everyone is going to experience this abundant life. We are going to have to make a decision to take it for ourselves. He went through so much for you and me. He has given us everything. Choose to respond to that love by accepting the gift He gave us.

"He becometh poor that dealeth with a slack hand: but the hand of the diligent maketh rich. He that gathereth in summer is a wise son: but he that sleepeth in harvest is a son that causeth shame. Blessings are upon the head of the just: but violence covers the mouth of the wicked. The memory of the just is blessed:"

Proverbs 10:4–7

There is so much here. You can take one phrase at a time and just think on it. You can have a slack hand in giving, which means you have a lazy hand; you are slow to give. You will become poor this way. The hand of the diligent will make them rich because they keep planting, keep giving, and keep obeying God's voice. To gather in the summer is wise. To be ready when the harvest time comes is wise. Don't be lazy; don't be slack—be ready. It will pay off. Blessings are on the head of the just, and they come from God, the maker of heaven and earth. Even the memory of the righteous is blessed.

"The labour of the righteous tendeth to life: the fruit of the wicked to sin."

Proverbs 10:16

Their labor tends to life because they are a blessed people. The righteous trust in their God. He is their Jehovah, their good Shepherd. Everything that they touch is blessed. They live in obedience to Him. Their heart is to serve and to bless. Their words are spoken in wisdom to bring life, so it makes sense that their labor tends only to life. Romans 8:5–6 says, "For they that are after the flesh do mind the things of the flesh; but they that are after the Spirit the things of the Spirit. For to be carnally minded is death; but to be spiritually minded is life and peace."

"The blessing of the LORD, it maketh rich, and he addeth no sorrow with it."

Proverbs 10:22

We can try to force circumstances to happen. We can struggle in our own strength, but when we trust the Lord's provision and patiently wait for His timing, we will experience His blessing in our lives. When He provides, the blessing is rich, and when we do it, we are so limited. There is no sorrow that comes with the Lord's blessing, only joy— unspeakable joy. It is He who makes us rich.

"By the blessing of the upright the city is exalted: but it is overthrown by the mouth of the wicked."

Proverbs 11:1

Wherever the blessed man is, everything around him will be blessed. If he works in a particular job, that business will see blessing and growth. His children will be blessed. Read through Deuteronomy 28 and discover the blessings we are to be walking in. Out of the upright come blessings. He should be speaking with the wisdom and mercy of God, representing God to others. Yes, even the city will be blessed because he is there; for he will be blessing his city and praying for his city. Not so with the wicked.

"There is that scattereth, and yet increaseth; and there is that withholdeth more than is meet, but it tendeth to poverty. The liberal soul shall be made fat: and he that watereth shall be watered also himself."

Proverbs 11:24–25

If we think of a garden again, we can get a clearer picture of this scripture. A farmer would not expect any garden to grow by wishing for it. He knows he must plant seed, and he realizes he must plant the seed of the vegetable that he wishes to harvest. This is exactly how the Kingdom of God operates; you give and plant in good soil, and you are sowing into eternity. God is the one who brings the increase and multiplies the seed sown. If you withhold, you will see no multiplication. It's an attitude of generosity that will cause blessing in all areas of your life. A stingy man is a man full of stress and fear.

"He that trusteth in his riches shall fall: but the righteous shall flourish as a branch."

Proverbs 11:28

It is the love of money that is the root of all evil. We were meant and made to trust our creator, God our Father. He loves when we trust Him. We were not made or meant to trust in anything created, whether it be a person, animal, or thing. They are only a creation just like us. They cannot come through for us, for they are temporary on this earth, just as we are. If we trust in God, we will be blessed. He will cause us to grow, to bloom as a lush and fruitful branch. All will see and praise our God!

"The fruit of the righteous is a tree of life; and he that winneth souls is wise. Behold, the righteous shall be recompensed in the earth…"

Proverbs 11:30–31

Many scriptures speak of our words, the fruit of our lips. The righteous speak words of life, planting good seed with their words. They speak the Word of God, which is good seed, full of power and life. That seed grows as we speak it. It grows in the hearts of men, bringing them to the Lord. As we do this, we are wise. Rather than wasting our words, we cause them to work for the good of the kingdom. We shall be recompensed in the earth, meaning we shall be rewarded and be in peace.

"The slothful man roasteth not that which he took in hunting: but the substance of a diligent man is precious."

Proverbs 12:27

Why would you not roast what you hunted? Because it was too much work? This means that you wouldn't eat. God gave us two arms and two legs. He gave us strength for a reason, as well as a mind to think. As we make a choice to use these things, we will reap the benefits of our labor. The substance of a diligent man is precious due to his diligence. Diligence means "constant and earnest effort to accomplish what is undertaken; persistent exertion of body or mind." Our work pays off.

"He that tilleth his land shall be satisfied with bread: but he that followeth vain persons is void of understanding."

Proverbs 12:11

Amplified:

"He who tills his land shall be satisfied with bread, but he who follows worthless pursuits is lacking in sense and is without understanding."

The bottom line is God gave us strength for a reason. While we look to Him for His wisdom and are led by His Spirit, we still must be willing to work. It is God who will bless our work and our efforts. But if we don't work, we won't eat. He can't bless nothing. God's way is that we grow and increase. We should be the most blessed people on this earth.

"A man's belly shall be satisfied with the fruit of his mouth; and with the increase of his lips shall he be filled. Death and life are in the power of the tongue: and they that love it shall eat the fruit thereof."

Proverbs 18:20–21

Just as you are filled with physical food by inserting it into your mouth and into your stomach, your life will be satisfied by the fruit of words that come out of your mouth. You will have what you speak. The same is true with the increase of the physical food we eat as we eat more and more and are filled. As you speak with your words and increase those words more and more, your life will show what you speak. You have power in your tongue for either life or death. It is your choice. If you speak death, thatis what you shall have. If you speak life, life is what you shall have. Now, when you love a particular fruit, you will probably be buying and eating that kind of fruit often. The more you give your tongue to speaking life, the sooner it may come. As you give yourself to His Word, to meditate on it day and night, so shall you have good success. You are loving that fruit; those good words that you are speaking will bring to life exactly what you speak. There is power in your tongue.

"He that hath pity upon the poor lendeth unto the LORD; and that which he hath given will he pay him again."

Proverbs 19:1

Amplified

"He who has pity on the poor lends to the LORD, and that which he has given He will repay to him."

When we give to the poor, it is from God's heart. It is His heart to bless them and to give to them. We are His hands. His compassion moves on us. So you can think of it as a loan; as you give to the poor, God will give back to you.

"The thoughts of the diligent tend only to plenteousness; but of every one that is hasty only to want."

Proverbs 21:5

This is because a diligent person does not procrastinate. Instead, they think ahead and anticipate. They don't even waste their thoughts. They know that time is precious, and much time can be wasted just by thinking on nothing, whether it be cares, anxieties, or any of the things of this world. The diligent plan, sow, and reap using kingdom principles and the wisdom of God. They seek God and His thoughts. The hasty never consult God. They look to their own wisdom. In the end, they always fall short.

"A faithful man shall abound with blessings…"

Proverbs 28:20

We read many scriptures regarding sowing and reaping. A righteous man who is faithful in sowing continually shall also reap continually. We know that seed multiplies, and so it is a law that as he sows with a cheerful heart into good soil, he shall have an abundance of harvest. It's only a matter of time. Give, and it shall be given.

"For I will pour water upon him that is thirsty, and floods upon the dry ground: I will pour my spirit upon thy seed, and my blessing upon thine offspring."

Isaiah 44:3

God is the one who waters, feeds, and blesses. Blessing originated from our God. He doesn't curse; He blesses. When our thirst is quenched, we should thank God. When our dry ground is watered and nourished, we give thanks where thanks is due—our Creator. He pours his Spirit on our seed, which is our children. He is the one who blesses our offspring. It is a natural progression, and we should anticipate it, welcoming His blessing and always thanking Him for it.

Meditations 3 – I Am Loved

For now, I will simply state some scriptures that explain the importance of meditating and renewing your mind on the Holy Scriptures—two from the Old Testament and one from the New Testament.

"But his delight is in the law of the LORD; and in his law doth he meditate day and night. And he shall be like a tree planted by the rivers of water, that bringeth forth his fruit in his season; his leaf also shall not wither; and whatsoever he doeth shall prosper."

Psalm 1:2–3

"My son, attend to my words; incline thine ear unto my sayings. Let them not depart from thine eyes; keep them in the midst of thine heart. For they are life unto those that find them, and health to all their flesh."

Proverbs 4:20–22

"I beseech you therefore, brethren, by the mercies of God, that ye present your bodies a living sacrifice, holy, acceptable unto God, which is your reasonable service. And be not conformed to this world: but be ye transformed by the renewing of your mind, that ye may prove what is that good, and acceptable, and perfect, will of God."

Romans 12:1–2

It is not a waste of time to put your thoughts and your mind on God's Word—quite the opposite. You will be doing well for yourself, your body, your mind, and your future. It is rather a waste of time to worry and to only see and think on the problem or to dwell on the hopeless circumstances. Now, that really is a waste of time and can only bring death.

"We love because he first loved u."

1 John 4:16–21

He began to pursue you. It was His idea first. It was His idea to create you and His idea to love and chase you. When we know God loves us, a security comes over us. We are loved. A peace enters our hearts. Someone has pursued us. Someone loves us. This will cause a joy to rise up in us, where we will overflow and want to share His love with others.

"Because the love of God is shed abroad in our hearts by the Holy Ghost which is given to us."

Romans 5:5

Amplified:

"For God's love has been poured out in our hearts through the Holy Spirit Who has been given to us."

The Holy Spirit is God's gift to us and is a blessing to us in so many ways. One of these blessings is that the love of God has been poured into your heart. Sometimes a person can say, "I don't think I can love. It's too hard to love people that are mean." But really, God's love is in us through the Holy Spirit. We have His love. It is in us to partake of. You have all the love you need, for you and for others. So now, walk in it by faith. Begin to use it like you have it.

"Love never fails."

1 Corinthians 13:8

What the world needs now is love, but not just any love: the love of God as He gave His precious, only Son. Jesus gave Himself. He poured out His life, His love. Love restores and heals. When you encounter hard-to-love people, remember that the right way to treat them is with the love of God and that love will not fail. You can also look at it another way: God loves you and will never fail. He will never stop loving you. His love will never fail. You can meditate on these words forever, and each time you will see something new because His Words are alive.

"Yet the LORD will command his lovingkindness in the daytime, and in the night his song shall be with me, and my prayer unto the God of my life."

Psalm 42:8

Other Bible versions say, "By day the LORD directs his love." Sometimes we have our minds on problems or the cares of this world and we miss looking at the good that God has done. This says, "by day," which means every day.

"Follow the way of love."

1 Corinthians 14:1

This is the road we are supposed to take. We follow this way. This is actually a narrow way. Matthew 7:14 says, "Narrow is the way, which leadeth unto life, and few there be that find it." The way to life is through the love of God. As we love, we will find more life. There will be more peace. The way of love, remember, is a choice, not a feeling. We choose each day to love. We bite our tongue to keep out of trouble. It pleases God because that is how He loves. Do as your Father does.

"Thou shewest lovingkindness unto thousands…"
Jeremiah 32:18

God gets such a bad reputation sometimes; Satan spreads the lie that He is cruel and does evil acts. This scripture explains totally the opposite. He shows kindness because of His love—not just to a few but to thousands. The motive behind it in His heart is because He dearly loves you. He is the one who is full of compassion. He doesn't look at how imperfect you are; He wants to show kindness because He loves with an unconditional love, not a keeping score kind of love—you do good for me, then I'll love you. No. He spreads His love—just because.

"Fear not: for I have redeemed thee, I have called thee by thy name; thou art mine."
Isaiah 43:1

I used to read this in such a negative way due to not knowing the love of God; I thought He wanted to own me, to take my life from me and make me do things I didn't want to, like travel to Africa or the farthest places. I was very ignorant. It's not that way at all. Now I see this verse like this: When no one wants you, and they reject you, don't be afraid. I will never say that to you. I want you. I love you. I will be glad to call you my own. I will be glad to care for you. I know you. I will even call you by your name. You're not just a number; you're my precious creation.

"I, even I, am he that blotteth out thy transgressions for mine own sake, and will not remember thy sins."

Isaiah 43:25

Blot means to erase, to wipe away. God Himself has made a decision to erase your transgressions. He has decided to not even remember them. How many of us can do that? He does it for His own sake because He is a God of mercy and forgiveness. I also remember another scripture that goes with this: Psalm 103:12, which says, "As far as the east is from the west, so far hath he removed our transgressions from us." He's not looking for things that are wrong in you. He's looking for what's right. And that is what His son Jesus paid for. We stand in Jesus, and that is what God sees.

"Observe how Christ loved us. His love was not cautious but extravagant. He didn't love in order to get something from us but to give everything of himself to us. Love like that."

Ephesians 5:2, MSG

King James Version:

"And walk in love, as Christ also hath loved us, and hath given himself for us an offering and a sacrifice to God for a sweet smelling savor."

Love, real agape love, does not even consider one's self. It risks being hurt, being taken for granted, and being taken advantage of. God's love doesn't play it safe. He gives and gives and gives, lavishly, while throwing caution to the wind. This is the way He wants His children to live, pouring ourselves out just as Jesus did. Give and it shall be given unto you. The acts of Jesus were done with a right heart, which rose up high into heaven as a sweet smell to His Father.

"Let the beloved of the LORD rest secure in him, for he shields him all day long, and the one the LORD loves rests between his shoulders."

Deuteronomy 33:12

This verse was speaking of a son, Benjamin, but we can take it for us as well. You are the beloved of the Lord. And if the God of the universe sees you this way, as His beloved, then surely you should be secure in your heart. Why should I worry about anything? He loves me.

The security of His love will shield you all day long. The next part is very special: The one that the Lord loves rests between His shoulders. What is that? Between the shoulders is the heart, and you, dear one, are in His heart. When He thinks of you, it is with an endearing love, not a sorry obligation. He does not regret one thing He suffered for you.

"Behold, what manner of love the Father hath bestowed upon us, that we should be called the sons of God:"

1 John 3:1

Behold means to look on, to gaze on. And what manner means what kind. What kind of love is this? The God of the universe is a Father indeed. And He has given us so much love that He has called us His sons, His children. He has made this possible by adopting us and accepting us as His own. How can we understand this? It is something too wonderful to grasp.

"Hereby perceive we the love of God, because he laid down his life for us: and we ought to lay our lives for the brethren."

1 John 3:16

This is how we see His love; this is how we understand it. Because He laid his life down for us, we can lay our lives down for the brethren. To wrap your brain around this is astounding and takes tremendous humility. It takes a laying down of all pride and self-will. We could only do this if we really had a revelation of His love for us. We can only do this through His strength and His power and grace. I can begin, in small ways, to put myself aside. The more I do this, the easier it will become. God's love puts others first and yourself last.

"For the Father himself loveth you, because ye have loved me, and have believed that I came out from God."

John 16:27

When someone is kind to my children and watches out for them, I appreciate it. I see this scripture as saying this as well. In other translations, it states that the Father Himself tenderly loves you. First of all, He is a Father.

God the Creator is a Father! And He's our Father.

Because you believe in Jesus and love Jesus, the Father tenderly loves you. This type of love is called "phileo" in the Greek. It means to be a friend, to be fond of, and to have affection for.

"The LORD thy God in the midst of thee is mighty; he will save, he will rejoice over thee with joy; he will rest in his love, he will joy over thee with singing."

Zephaniah 3:17

New International Reader's Version:

"The LORD your God is with you. He is mighty enough to save you. He will take great delight in you. The quietness of his love will calm you down. He will sing with joy because of you."

I love the version above in the NIRV. I believe it is speaking of Jesus. It says in verse 15, "The LORD hath taken away thy judgments, he hath cast out thine enemy: the king of Israel, even the LORD, is in the midst of thee: thou shalt not see evil any more."

And now He is in the midst of you, if you are saved. He is mighty in you to save; He has become the curse for you and defeated the enemy. He has taken great delight in you and rejoiced in you. He has rescued and saved you because He loves you, not because He had to. He chose to. He is excited about you. Some just can't see this, but it is here in the Word, and it is the truth. "He will rest in his love." I see this in my heart as twofold. When Christ finished His work, He went to heaven and sat at the right hand of God. Mark 16:19 says that because of His love for us, He finished the work and then rested. He completed the work.

The other idea is that when you are in the midst of a storm or overcome by turbulence and anxiety, doubt, or fear, to be still…and let His love calm you. Picture the face of Jesus, and let His love for you bring peace to your heart. Here is where I picture a wild stallion that only the master of that horse can tame and calm; only his own whisper into the horse's ear can bring him to a hushed calm.

"Can a mother forget the baby at her breast and have no compassion on the child she has borne? Though she may forget, I will not forget you! See, I have engraved you on the palms of my hands: your walls are ever before me."

Isaiah 49:15–16

If only the world were full of good mothers. We know that the fact is that this is not so, and it is a shame, but one thing we can be sure of is this: God the Father will never forget you. God is your Father, and He will always have compassion on you, for you are His child.

A good father loves his kids and has mercy on them. Why, He even says, "See." See and look at His hands. Use your imagination and picture them. He says to you that He has engraved you on the palms of His hands. Sweethearts engrave and carve their names on a tree, hoping it will be there for life. They are telling each other, and the world, that they belong together, that they love each other. This reminds me of the holes in the hands of Jesus. His nail-scarred hands don't remind Him of the terrible pain He suffered. Instead, they remind Him of His love for you and how precious you are to Him.

Jesus is God come in the flesh. Your walls are ever before Him. Yes, this is speaking of the walls of Jerusalem. But it is also speaking of us. Now let's think about this: Walls are for protection. Now that we are in Christ, He is our protection; He is our shepherd.

"And call no man your father upon the earth: for one is your father, which is in heaven."

Matthew 23:9

Just as there are good and bad mothers, the same is true with fathers. We are all human, and if people did not grow up knowing and learning about God and His Word, they only know the ways of the world. However, regardless of good or bad, kind or mean, we must look to God as our real Father. The fact that He is a Father is amazing. The fact that He wants to be our Father is even more amazing. This means we have a family. A real family. One day we will see Him face to face, but for now, yes, you can enjoy Him, for He lives in you. He hears you and sees you, and if you listen to His still, small voice, you will hear Him.

"Mercy triumphs over judgment.

James 2:13 (NIV)

Message:

"Kind mercy wins over harsh judgment every time."

Wherever you look in this world, there is judgment and pointing fingers. The world seems to enjoy and even be entertained by people falling and making mistakes. There are talk shows, sitcoms, reality shows, and magazines full of gossip proclaiming, "Look who fell today." This all comes from Satan. He criticizes. He is the god of this world. He accuses the Christian and condemns us with constant guilt.

If you remember, wherever Jesus went on the earth, people would say, "Have mercy on me." They knew He had and showed mercy, for He showed love; He healed and delivered. This is our kingdom; this is where we need to live. Through the mercy of God, Jesus overcame judgment. In fact, He triumphed over judgment.

"I will never leave thee, nor forsake thee. So that we may boldly say, The Lord is my helper, and I will not fear what man shall do unto me."

Hebrews 13:5–6

Amplified:

"For He [God] Himself has said, I will not in any way fail you nor give you up nor leave you without support. [I will] not, [I will] not, [I will] not in any degree leave you helpless nor forsake nor let [you] down (relax My hold on you)! [Assuredly not!] So we take comfort and are encouraged and confidently and boldly say, The Lord is my Helper; I will not be seized with alarm [I will not fear or dread or be terrified]. What can man do to me?"

One of the main lies that the devil shouts to us is that we are alone. No one loves us. God has left us. These are out-and-out lies from Satan. Remember, he is the father of lies. This is a great scripture to memorize and meditate on often so that when a trial comes, one of the first things you can tell yourself is "I'm not alone. God is with me and for me." People may give up on you because they are human; they may not know the unconditional love of God. Friends will leave you and not support you. Spouses may leave. Parents may leave. But God is perfect. God is love. He never changes, and He is the biggest promise keeper in the universe. He will never let go of you. He loves watching over you. Believe His Word!

"For the mountains shall depart, and the hills be removed; but my kindness shall not depart from thee, neither shall the covenant of my peace be removed, saith the LORD that hath mercy on thee."

Isaiah 54:10

Amplified:

"For though the mountains should depart and the hills be shaken or removed, yet my love and kindness shall not depart from you, nor shall My covenant of peace and completeness be removed, says the Lord, Who has compassion on you."

Message:

"For even if the mountains walk away and the hills fall to pieces, my love won't walk away from you, my covenant commitment of peace won't fall apart. The GOD who has compassion on you says so."

When we read about mountains shaking and hills being removed, this is speaking about our crazy, overwhelming circumstances. They are always changing. We can never count on them staying the same. In fact, all the things your eyes see in the physical realm are subject to change. Don't hold onto them. They will let you down. His love for you will never end. Nothing can change how He feels about you, and nothing you can do will stop Him from loving you. Because of the covenant that Jesus made on our behalf with God, all of this is so. This covenant is unbreakable; it is sure. How can God break an agreement with Himself? This is a God of compassion we are speaking about. And it is God Himself who is stating this. These words are coming out of His own mouth. Because of Jesus, you have everlasting peace with God.

"For God so loved the world that he gave his only begotten Son, that whosoever believeth in him should not perish, but have everlasting life."

John 3:16

Amplified:

"For God so greatly loved and dearly prized the world, that he [even] gave up His only begotten (unique) Son, so that whoever believes in (trusts in, clings to, relies on) Him shall not perish (come to destruction, be lost) but have eternal (everlasting) life."

Sometimes we can overlook such a famous scripture. You've heard it tons of times before. I challenge you to look with new eyes. God is not cruel. God does not play games with people's lives. God is love. This verse does not say God loves the world. It says He SO loved the world. That little, tiny word makes a difference. This means "very much"—so much that He did something about it. But wait. It says He loved the world. Who does this include?

Does it leave anyone out? Not one.

Which one of us would give our child that we treasure for anyone else? This is how vast God's love is. Who can comprehend this kind of love that is free to all but costs the giver everything? He is saying, if you believe in my Son, you will never perish but have everlasting life.

God was willing to save us from our destruction. No one else could save us. We could not save ourselves even. Oh, the love of God…what a beautiful thing it is. When we have Jesus living in us, we have His love living in us as well. This means we can love this same way if we give ourselves to it. Surrender to His love, and give up your will and your selfishness. To live and stay in this mind of love is what true life is all about. It is the highest life there is.

"Love is patient, love is kind. It does not envy, it does not boast, it is not proud. It does not dishonor others, it is not self-seeking, it is not easily angered, it keeps no record of wrongs. Love does not delight in evil but

rejoices with the truth. It always protects, always trusts, always hopes, always perseveres. Love never fails."

1 Corinthians 13:4–8 (NIV)

This is the God kind of love. This is God's character. This is how God loves you and me and all the world. Let's read it as so:

God is patient with me. He is kind with me. He does not envy. He doesn't brag, and He isn't full of pride. God does not dishonor me or others. He is not self-seeking; He is not easily angered. God keeps no record of wrongs. He doesn't focus on and remind me of my mistakes. God does not delight in evil or when bad things happen to me, but He rejoices with the truth. He always protects me, always trusts me, always hopes in me, and always perseveres. He is my biggest cheerleader. His love for me never fails.

"How excellent is thy lovingkindness, O God! therefore the children of men put their trust under the shadow of thy wings. They shall be abundantly satisfied with the fatness of thy house; and thou shalt make them drink of the river of thy pleasures. For with thee is the fountain of life: in thy light shall we see light. O continue thy lovingkindness unto them that know thee; and thy righteousness to the upright in heart."

Psalm 36:7–10

The love of God is so great! We as His children can come and hide under the shadow of His wings. We can trust Him and His protection and provision because we know He loves us. We are confident in that love. We come into His presence to worship, and we come expecting because we trust Him. We know we will walk away full. We will be nourished, fed, refreshed, and overflowing when we come into His presence. We won't be just satisfied. We are sure to be abundantly satisfied. He will make us drink of the river of His pleasures. He has nothing but life and goodness to give.

With Him is the fountain of life! Picture yourself near a beautiful fountain. Imagine the spray of it on you, so refreshing. You can come into His presence any time you want to. Because of Jesus, you now have an open invitation. We are the ones who can stray away from Him. He never leaves or strays away from us. We will see His light as we walk in that light. First John 2:10–11 says that when you walk in God's love, you are walking in the light. Because we know Him, He will continue His lovingkindness toward us.

"God is love."

1 John 4:8

Even though this is a very short phrase, as you get more familiar with meditating on the Scriptures and are led by the Holy Spirit, you will find that this phrase can speak volumes. It ties in with so many other scriptures.

This verse could have said God is joy or God is peace. We know He has these qualities, but it doesn't say that. It says God is love. He is not hate. He is not cruel. He is full of mercy and forgiveness. These stem from His love. Peace and joy stem from His love. If He doesn't change, like it says in James 1:17, then He has always been love. This means that love always was. That love created the earth. It was love that created Adam. And the motivation to make man was love.

"God is love; and he that dwelleth in love dwelleth in God, and God in him."

1 John 4:16

A child learns what they live with from their parents. Good habits and bad habits. In this case, there are no bad habits with God. He is love. And as we follow Him and His ways, we will be love. We must give ourselves to this love. We surrender to it. It is a choice, not a feeling. And notice the word "dwell." This means to live, to stay. So in other words, you don't come to it when it's convenient or when you're feeling compassionate and merciful. You stay. You stay and live there through thick and through thin. This is your home, for this is God's home. People will see this love that is so fantastically different from anything else they've seen. The world has nothing like it and never will.

"According as he has chosen us in him before the foundation of the world, that we should be holy and without blame before him in love."

Ephesians 1:4

This verse declares so much; it can never be described in a simple paragraph. You and I were a thought and a picture in His mind before He even created the world. Not only that but He saw your whole life all at once. He planned your life and a good life at that (Jer. 29:11). He chose us.

"But God, who is rich in mercy, for his great love wherewith he loved us."

Ephesians 2:4

Who can you say of anyone on this earth, "Ah, they are rich in mercy"? Maybe some mature Christians will have much mercy as they choose to live there. But even they are only human. Yes, we have Christ living in us, but we still live in this fleshly body, and we still get physically tired. But God never gets tired, never sleeps, and never grows weary. He is truly rich in mercy and compassion, forgiveness and goodness. We see people who are rich in bank accounts. God is rich in mercy, meaning He has plenty of mercy to go around; He will never run out. He has so much that in His great love, He chose to love you and me

"Who shall separate us from the love of Christ? Shall tribulation, or distress, or persecution, or famine, or nakedness, or peril, or sword?"

Romans 8:35

Nothing on this earth, no matter how bad or how extreme, that we go through can ever stop His love to us. This is what He does. He loves, He is love, and He will keep loving throughout eternity. Christ loved us in our wretched sin. He died for us when we were at our worst. And even when you get saved and slip into sin, still you cannot stop Him from loving you. You may hide in your guilt and choose not to run to Him, but His arms are always open, for He has paid for your forgiveness. Dare to run into the arms of His never-ending love.

"Nay, in all these things we are more than conquerors through him that loved us."

Romans 8:37

In all these things—meaning tribulation, distress, persecution, famine, nakedness, peril, sword, etc.—we still come out on top. He defeated sin, defeated Satan. Jesus is the victor, and we get to partake in that victory.

In fact, we are more than conquerors because we didn't have to do a thing except believe and receive Him as our Lord and Savior. He did the work, and He causes us to reap the benefits! He is so good and so loving to us even when we surely don't deserve it.

"I in them, and thou in me, that they may be made perfect in one; and that the world may know that thou hast sent me, and hast loved them, as thou hast loved me."

John 17:23

His prayer to His Father and our Father is that we should be one in Him and in each other. One. No divisions, no unforgiveness. One body. Nourishing and nurturing each other, preferring one another. There should be such a difference in us that the world will see it and will know clearly that we are different.

They should know that God the Father loves us and loved Jesus. Sometimes we walk around not realizing that Christ really lives in us. We forget about that. He sees what we see, feels what we feel, and hears what we hear, and He wants us to become aware of that. He wants us to become aware of His deep love for us—that it would envelope us so much that we would walk in that same love for each other.

"Shew thy marvelous lovingkindness, O thou that savest by thy right hand them which put their trust in thee from those that rise up against them."

Psalm 17:7

When He shows up in your life and rescues you or protects and saves you from evil situations, you can be sure that He is showing His marvelous lovingkindness. He is doing it because He loves you. He is doing this because you are trusting Him. He loves when His kids trust Him. He loves to show forth His strength like a good Father. You can picture a dad coming to his child's school and showing up to face the bully that picked on his child. He is glad to protect and defend. God is a strong, loving Father, and He is no different; in fact, He is even more protective.

"Remember, O LORD, thy tender mercies and thy loving kindnesses; for they have been ever of old."

Psalm 25:6

The tender mercies and lovingkindness of God have always been. To us they are from old, but they actually have always been in existence because God has always been. He is the Alpha and Omega, the great I AM. He will never run out. We will be experiencing his lovingkindness throughout time and for all eternity. We will be amazed over and over again at how great His love is toward us.

"For thy lovingkindness is before mine eyes: and I have walked in thy truth."

Psalm 26:3

Sometimes we can wake up on the wrong side of the bed and miss seeing His goodness throughout the day. It's much easier for people to see the negative and the things that are not perfect—the things that are not done—than to see the good side. You must get in the habit of opening your eyes and looking on the good. Open your eyes and see His lovingkindness; see even the little blessings that come your way throughout your day. You walk outside and hear a bird singing a simple song. Don't take things for granted. Think about it. That bird is actually singing praises to God, for that is how God made him. Let everything that hath breath praise the Lord, the psalmist wrote. Watch for His lovingkindness. When you walk in His truth and keep His truth in your mind, you will see His lovingkindness.

"I have not concealed thy lovingkindness and thy truth from the great congregation."

Psalm 40:10

The world needs to know this great, loving God. The Church needs to know of His lovingkindness. We can plant seeds and share of His goodness. Sometimes their eyes can also be closed to seeing His love. God can use us to share with them; we must not hide it and keep it all to ourselves. The world is starving for love. Spread the good news.

"Withhold not thou thy tender mercies from me, O LORD: let thy lovingkindness and thy truth continually preserve me."

Psalm 40:11

We can surely see in the New Testament that He has not withheld anything from us. He has given us everything that pertains to life and godliness (1 Peter 1:3). He has given us Jesus. His lovingkindness and His truth have beengiven freely to us. His Word sanctifies us (John 17:17) and washes over our minds as we give ourselves to it, renewing our thoughts. His Word preserves us continually.

"Because thy lovingkindness is better than life, my lips shall praise thee."

Psalm 63:3

Life is good in itself, but it does not compare to the life we can have with the Lord. He is the source of our life and the reason we sing—the reason we love and laugh. His lovingkindness is so sweet that it is better than life. Life will one day end on this earth, and He will create a new heaven and a new earth. But His lovingkindness will never end; it will always be. Because He has given you and me new life, we will always be. Forever my lips shall praise Him for all the kindness He has shown to me. He didn't have to give me eternal life, but He did. And even more, He has welcomed us to live with Him as His children forever. My lips shall praise You my God, my Father, my Jesus, my Savior!

"Also I will make him my firstborn, higher than the kings of the earth. My mercy will I keep for him for evermore, and my covenant shall stand fast with him. His seed also will I make to endure for ever, and his throne as the days of heaven."

Psalm 89:27–29

Jesus is God come in the flesh. Romans 8:11 speaks of how the Spirit raised Christ from the dead. He is higher than any king on the earth; He is the King of kings and the Lord of Lords. Every benefit that Jesus has been given we can partake of if we are in Him. God said He will keep His mercy for him forevermore, and the same goes for us in Christ. God made a covenant with Jesus that will last forever. It will never break. We can always enjoy this covenant of peace; it will never end. How can it end if Jesus made the covenant with God? Perfect plus perfect equals perfect. His seed is speaking of us. That we could live forever and ever in peace with the Father Almighty, with Jesus and the Holy Spirit, is amazing. We are blessed beyond measure.

"To shew forth thy lovingkindness in the morning, and thy faithfulness every night."

Psalm 92:2

If we realize it and open our eyes to it, we can see His lovingkindness every morning. When the sun comes up and shines on everything and everyone, that alone is a blessing. It's the time when all creation begins to sing and rejoice. I remember one morning sitting in my backyard drinking my coffee and meditating on Scripture, worshiping Jesus, and I looked up and sat still. All of a sudden, I became aware of my surroundings, which were very busy: bees buzzing back and forth, hummingbirds stopping to flutter on a flower, and dragonflies flying above, all mixed with grasshoppers and butterflies. If you think about it, yes, they are busy working on finding food, but they are also praising their Creator because they are doing what they were designed to do. A new day equals new mercies. And by the end of the day, after you have seen your Father answering prayers and using you to be a blessing, you can thank Him at night for His faithfulness.

"Who redeemeth thy life from destruction; who crowneth thee with lovingkindness and tender mercies;

Psalm 103:4

I believe that when we get to heaven, we will hear and find out all of the many stories of where the Lord rescued and saved us from harm. He not only redeems us but He crowns us with lovingkindness. We did not deserve any kindness, but He did it anyway because of His great love.

"I will worship toward thy holy temple, and praise thy name for thy lovingkindness and for thy truth: for thou hast magnified thy word above all thy name."

Psalm 138:2

When I think about the words "toward thy holy temple," I am reminded that in the Old Testament, this is where God's presence was. But now, in the New Testament, through the finished work of Christ, His presence is in us every day and from now on and forever. I will worship Him anywhere, anytime. That it would give Him joy to be kind to us and that He loves to do this for His children means He is such a good Father, a good God. I can worship Him for His truth, and we know that His truth is His Word. His truth is full of life to us. His truth sets us free. In Psalm 107:20 it mentions that He sent His word and healed them. We know that His Word is Jesus. We also read that from John 1:14: And the Word was made flesh and dwelt among us, and we beheld his glory.

It reminds me of Philippians 2:9–10, where it says God has highly exalted Him and given Him a name that is above every name. Jesus went to the lowest depths, and God then chose to exalt Him higher than any name.

"The LORD hath appeared of old unto me, saying, Yea, I have loved thee with an everlasting love: therefore with lovingkindness have I drawn thee."

Jeremiah 31:3

If the love of God is everlasting, that means it always was, even before we were and created. And His love is everlasting, meaning it will never end or even run out. His love for me is forever. He has drawn me with lovingkindness not cruelty or the pointing of the finger, telling me of all my mistakes and failures. Romans 2:4 says it's the goodness of God that leads men to repentance. When a person comes to us and points out our wrongs and tells us how to do it right, we are not encouraged but more likely pushed away. Yet when someone comes to you and points out your good points and compliments you with honesty and sincerity, you are blessed and want to go the extra mile for them. God is this way. Jesus didn't come to condemn the world but to save it.

"And I will betroth thee unto me for ever; yea, I will betroth thee unto me in righteousness, and in judgment, and in lovingkindness, and in mercies."

Hosea 2:19

This verse also proves the one before it. He didn't woo us with cruelty and punishment or with manipulative control and anger. He wooed us with mercies and in righteousness. Jesus gave Himself for us, and He loved us first. He wants us. And He wants us for His own. He wanted to betroth us to Him forever. This relationship will always be new and never get old and worn out. He is a righteous, fair judge, full of forgiveness and mercy.

"I have heard your prayer and seen your tears."

2 Kings 20:5 (NIV)

Sometimes, or I should say many times, we think God has forgotten us. We see Him at times as far away and that He doesn't know what we are going through and couldn't possibly understand our circumstances. But that is wrong and actually a lie. He knows and sees everything. Nothing gets past our God. He hears our prayers. He has seen every single one of your tears that you have cried in private, even when you thought no one cared.

"Thou tellest my wanderings: put thou my tears into thy bottle: are they not in thy book?"

Psalm 56:8

How much love and compassion does this God have? This is the Father of mercies and God of all comfort.

(**2 Corinthians 1:3**).

Think of all the tears you've ever cried throughout your entire life: when you were a baby and then a child; as you went through your school years; as you grew up and got married; as your life may have not turned out as you wanted it to or thought and planned it would. You may have had many disappointments in life. Things and people may have not been fair to you. But God your Father saw it all. And He knew about every single one of your tears. This verse says He even saved them in His bottle. He cares more than you or I know. I believe when we get to heaven, we will be so surprised when we are able to see clearly for ourselves how much He cares for each one of us. No one person is cared for more than the other. We are all equally His favorite.

Meditations 4 –
I'm In Christ

This chapter will outline what it means to be in Christ and the promises that brings. We will be meditating on scriptures that speak of our identity in Him as well as those that will illustrate why He has allowed us to live in Him—because He loves us.

"I will greatly rejoice in the LORD, my soul shall be joyful in my God; for he hath clothed me with the garments of salvation, he hath covered me with the robe of righteousness, as a bridegroom decketh himself with ornaments, and as a bride adorneth herself with jewels."

Isaiah 61:10

This is in the Old Testament, yet it is very prophetic of Jesus. We can greatly rejoice in the Lord; we can choose joy. Soul, you shall be joyful in your God! Look what He has done! To be clothed with the garments of salvation is to receive what Jesus has done for you. He has forgiven our sins and put us in right standing with God; we now have peace with God. He is the one who did it by His grace. We could not do this for ourselves. He has covered me with the robe of righteousness. We are the bride which is the Church, getting ready for our bridegroom Jesus. He has made us beautiful. Philippians 1:6 says, "Being confident of this very thing, that he which has begun a good work in me, will perform it until the day of Jesus Christ."

"And by him all that believe are justified from all things, from which ye could not be justified by the law of Moses."

Acts 13:39

The law of Moses was the Ten Commandments. It could not justify us; it only magnified our sins. No one could keep the law—only one, and that is Jesus. As we believe in Him, by Him we are justified in all things before God. There is no more guilt or condemnation to those who are in Christ Jesus, who walk not after the flesh but after the Spirit (Romans 8:1).

"Being justified freely by his grace through redemption that is in Christ Jesus."

Romans 3:24

Christ has redeemed us. He has redeemed us from the curse of the law, and He did it by His grace. Grace is what you cannot do for yourself. No one can redeem themselves; it is impossible. He did it for free out of an enduring love for us. I am justified freely just as if I'd never sinned. To be given His grace is very humbling. It shows His great love and mercy toward man.

"And not only so, but we also joy in God through our Lord Jesus Christ, by whom we now received the atonement."

Romans 5:11

God is our Father—the great and merciful Father. It is through Jesus and His work on the cross that we have peace with God—that we are adopted by God and that we now can have joy in God the Father. We who have been saved now have a right to come to God in peace and joy, rejoicing in Him as our Father. It is through Jesus that we now have received atonement, which is restoration and reconciliation with God.

"Know ye not, that so many of us as were baptized into Jesus Christ were baptized into his death?

Romans 6:3

This verse starts out with a question: "Know ye not?" Don't you know? Don't you realize? Those who have accepted Jesus Christ as their Lord and Savior were given new life, but in order to have new life, one has to die first. He died for us all, but in His death, we also died. We were baptized into life with Him and into death with Him. We now have a newnature that is one with God's Spirit. The Spirit of God lives in us, and His power and anointing are inside of us to stay, never to leave, regardless of how you feel. We need to awaken to this revelation.

"Likewise reckon ye also yourselves to be dead indeed unto sin, but alive unto God through Jesus Christ our Lord."

Romans 6:11

Reckon means to take an inventory, to estimate. See yourselves as truly dead to sin. You are for sure dead to sin if you are in Christ. But just as much as you are dead, you also truly are alive unto God through Jesus Christ our Lord. We look too much to the circumstances in front of us. 2 Corinthians 4:18 says:

"While we look not at the things which are seen, but at the things which are not seen: for the things which are seen are temporal; but the things which are not seen are eternal." We should look deeper and see what God sees. See things as they really are, not what we see. We are alive unto God! We have the power of God inside of us that raised Christ from the dead!

"There is therefore now no condemnation to them which are in Christ Jesus, who walk not after the flesh, but after the Spirit."

Romans 8:1

Right now, this moment, there is no guilt. Any guilt that you are feeling is not coming from God. Because of Christ, He does not see you as guilty, but you must first accept Him. He took your sin on His back; He took your guilt and your shame. Second Corinthians 5:21 says, "For he hath made him to be sin for us, who knew no sin; that we might be made the righteousness of God in him." When you are in Christ, you are dead to the flesh, so you have no need to walk after it anymore. Your flesh does not have power over you any longer, unless you let it. Your spirit is now alive so that you can walk after the Spirit of life, which is in Christ.

"And if Christ be in you, the body is dead because of sin; but the Spirit is life because of righteousness."

Romans 8:10

You are the righteousness of God in Christ Jesus. What we could not do on our own Christ did for us.No one is twisting our arms any more to sin. We were sinners. We were all born into sin, but through the work of Jesus, we have been made saints. Jesus did it. When we get baptized in water, it is a sign to show others what has happened on the inside. We were buried and have been raised into new life in Christ Jesus. Old things have passed away; behold all things are new. If the body is dead tosin, so be it. If you put vodka in front of a dead man who used to be an alcoholic, how can he drink it if he is dead? Now the only way we sin is if we choose to. Now we are free from sin. Choose life!

"For I am persuaded, that neither death nor life, nor angels, nor principalities, nor powers, nor things present, nor things to come, nor height, nor depth, nor any other creature, shall be able to separate us from the love of God, which is in Christ Jesus our Lord."

Romans 8:38–39

The great love of God is in Christ Jesus our Lord. One reason is that Jesus is God. God the Father, Jesus, and the Holy Spirit are one. First John 5:7 says, "For there are three that bear record in heaven, the Father, the Word, and the Holy Ghost: and these three are one." God also loves His Son Jesus very much, yet God loves us the same as He loves Jesus. They are one, and we are one. There is nothing that can separate us from the love of God—nothing. His love is in our Spirit. We are one; it can never leave, for His Spirit is joined with our Spirit now. No death can separate you from His love—not life nor angels; no darkness, principalities, or powers can separate you from the love of God. No past, no present, no future can do it. No height, no depth can separate you. No creature, animal, or person shall ever be able to separate you from His love. There is nothing that you can do or have ever done that will stop God from loving you.

"So we, being many, are one body in Christ, and every one members one of another."

Romans 12:5

Think of the millions of Christians all over the world in many different countries: all of the diverse people groups with various races, colors, and languages, all coming from many walks of life— rich and poor, famous and unknown. All these make up one body with Christ being the head. In Christ, we are one. Each is a different member with different gifts and purposes, but we all need each other; we nurture and feed one another.

Without each other, there is no body. The same love is in each of our spirits. We have that love in common no matter how different we are. But it is because of Him. He brings us all together. He is our Lord. He is our head and chief cornerstone.

"I thank my God always on your behalf, for grace of God which is given you by Jesus Christ; That in every thing ye are enriched by him, in all utterance, and in all knowledge; Even as the testimony of Christ was confirmed in you: So that you come behind in no gift..."

1 Corinthians 1:4–7

Paul thanked God for His grace on our behalf, and that grace was given to us by Jesus Christ. We are enriched in everything in Jesus — from the words that come out of our mouths to all knowledge that we have been given. If you are saved, then His testimony has been confirmed in you. This truly describes His grace, for in His love and because of His love for you, He provided all that you would ever need in this life and into eternity with Him.

"Unto the church of God which is at Corinth, to them that are sanctified in Christ Jesus, called to be saints, with all that in every place call upon the name of Jesus Christ our Lord, both theirs and ours:"

1 Corinthians 1:2

Although this is about the Corinthian church, anyone who is in Christ is His church. We are the body of Christ. We also are sanctified because of Christ and are called to be saints. Sanctified means consecrated; to be holy is to be pure. There is no way we are capable of doing this ourselves. It is Christ who made us holy. We are called saints only due to the work of Christ. Hebrews 10:14 says, "For by one offering he hath perfected for ever them that are sanctified."

"But of Him are ye in Christ Jesus, who of God is made unto us wisdom, and righteousness, and sanctification, and redemption:"

Corinthians 1:30

The Amplified version says it this way:

"But it is from Him that you have your life in Christ Jesus, Whom God made our Wisdom from God, [revealed to us a knowledge of the divine plan of salvation previously hidden, manifesting itself as] our Righteousness [thus making us upright and putting us in right standing with God], and our Consecration [making us pure and holy], and our Redemption [providing our ransom from eternal penalty for sin]."

Every good and perfect gift comes from the Father. He is a good Father who takes good care of His children. He is a great provider and wanted to make sure that we would be taken care of spirit, soul, and body. He gave us everything in the physical and spiritual realm. Jesus is made unto us righteousness, sanctification, and redemption. It is because of Him that we have these gifts. In Christ, I am the righteousness of God and have right standing with God. In Christ, I am sanctified and have been made holy. In Christ, I have been redeemed; by the blood of the lamb I am saved. I have been bought back to my rightful owner. He ransomed me.

"For who hath known the mind of the Lord, that he may instruct him? but we have the mind of Christ."

1 Corinthians 2:16

No one can teach the Lord; He is all-knowing and all-seeing. To see inside the mind of God would be incredible. But we, who are in Christ, have the mind of Christ. We have access to all the wonderful things God has provided. We don't have to rely on our own limited resources. He is the vast creator. He is the one who created and developed the atom. Lean on Him; this provision, as we trust Him, is a blessing to us and for us and for all humanity.

"We are fools for Christ's sake, but ye are wise in Christ;"

1 Corinthians 4:10

We are fools for Christ's sake. This is to say we take our eyes off of ourselves and become Christ centered. We humble ourselves and lift up the name of Jesus. In Christ, we are wise. We put our own wisdom aside, for it does not compare with His wisdom.

"For as in Adam all die, even so in Christ shall all be made alive."

1 Corinthians 15:22

Adam sinned, and this brought death into the world. Every person then to be born would be born into sin, which in turn brought death. And in the same way, as Christ was made alive, this brought life to all, if they would receive Him. All shall be made alive. Death came through one, but much more life came through the one, Jesus Christ.

"Now thanks be unto God, which always causeth us to triumph in Christ, and maketh manifest the savour of his knowledge by us in every place."

1 Corinthians 2:14

Be thankful to God for His generous benefits. He always causes us to triumph in Christ, and to triumph is to have the victory. We must get our eyes off of the problem and the circumstances in order to do this (2 Corinthians 4:18).

"Jesus, when he had cried again with a loud voice, yielded up the ghost. And, behold, the veil of the temple was rent in twain from top to bottom; and the earth did quake, and the rocks rent; And the graves were opened; and many bodies of the saints which slept arose, and came out of the graves after his resurrection, and went into the holy city, and appeared unto many."

Matthew 27:50–53

What an amazing verse. This has so much to think and ponder on. When Jesus was on the cross, the very moment that He gave up the ghost the veil was torn. The gospel of John says that one of the last things that Jesus said was "It is finished." At once God tore the veil that was in the temple. He wanted His children to have complete access to His throne and to be able to come to Him freely. In the Old Testament, only the high priest could be in God's presence. After Jesus died on the cross, no more sacrifices were needed; His was the perfect sacrifice, and now all could come to God through Jesus. When the veil was torn, it was torn from the top, which man could not do.

"For he hath made him to be sin for us, who knew no sin; that we might be made the righteousness of God in him."

2 Corinthians 5:21

God the Father is the one who made Jesus to be sin for us. It was because of love that He made Jesus into sin. He poured the wrath that we really deserved onto Him that we might be made the righteousness of God in Him. He uses the word "might" because not everyone is going to take Him up on that. Many will not choose the love of God. Many hate God because of the spirit of the antichrist. He will let them go to hell if they choose, but many will choose the free gift of righteousness.

"Therefore if any man be in Christ, he is a new creature: old things are passed away; behold, all things are become new."

2 Corinthians 5:17

Your spirit man inside of you is a new creature if you are in Christ. Your spirit man was born into a sin nature because of Adam. We were all the same, and we had to receive Jesus when we first found out about Him. At that time, we became new creatures. God's Spirit became one with our spirit. A new creature is just that—brand new. Old things are passed away. That means all the past. Think of all of your past failures, mistakes, sickness, etc. You have a clean slate. Behold, look and see; all things are become new.

"I am crucified with Christ: nevertheless I live; yet not I, but Christ liveth in me: and the life which I now live in the flesh I live by the faith of the Son of God, who loved me, and gave himself for me."

Galatians 2:20

This first phrase sounds like an oxymoron, but it is speaking again about your spirit man. Your spirit man, the old sin nature, was crucified with Christ on the cross. Your new spirit, if you are in Christ, is the one who is now living; yet not you alone but Christ is the one who lives in you. And the body, the life you now live in the flesh, you live by the faith of Jesus. He is the one who loved you and gave Himself up for you. He gave you His faith to live.

"There is neither Jew nor Greek, there is neither bond nor free, there is neither male nor female: for ye are all one in Christ Jesus."

Galatians 3:28

When we are in Christ, we are His body.

When you bring all of us together who are in Christ, we are all His body—one body. Christ is the head. It doesn't matter who you are, or who you were, or even what gender you are. We all become one in Christ. We are one family, one body, one Lord. No one is higher than another. We are all loved equally. We need each other.

"For in Christ Jesus neither circumcision availeth any thing, nor uncircumcision, but a new creature."

Galatians 6:15

This new creature that we became when we received Christ is all due to His work and His performance on the cross. He did the work by grace and because of His love for us. We cannot brag about any significant work that we have done. It will not matter, and it will not match up to all that He has done. Remember, it is by grace you are saved and not of yourselves. It is a gift of God, not of works, lest any man should boast. The Old Testament law required that Jewish males be circumcised. This was out of obedience to God. But now in the New Testament, speaking of Christ dying on the cross for us, that is no longer necessary. The old is done away with. Now we have grace. It is by grace that we are saved and live. No work or act of any circumcision can save you but only the sacrifice of Jesus on the cross.

"Blessed be the God and Father of our Lord Jesus Christ, who hath blessed us with all spiritual blessings in heavenly places in Christ:

Ephesians 1:3

Jesus, through His cross and resurrection, provided everything we would ever need in this life and in eternity to come. Everything you see and touch was created first by the spiritual realm. Having all that we need in the spiritual blessings in heavenly places is primary because through the Spirit, you can speak forth by faith to receive of the physical realm. So having rights in the spiritual realm is crucial for subduing and taking our authority on this earth. So we can say, "Blessed be the God of our Lord Jesus Christ!" For He has done a great thing for us!

"In whom we have redemption through his blood, the forgiveness of sins, according to the riches of his grace;"

Ephesians 1:7

It is through the blood of Jesus that we have been redeemed. He shed His blood as an offering for our sins. He paid for our redemption in full. Nothing more is owed. You are free from the power of darkness. You are free from Satan's kingdom and from his hold. You are freed from hell forever. The precious price was high, but it was fully paid. All of your sins have been forgiven: past, present, and future. This is according to the riches of His grace.

"Even when we were dead in sins, hath quickened us together with Christ, (by grace ye are saved;) And hath raised us up together, and made us sit together in heavenly places in Christ Jesus. That in the ages to come he might shew the exceeding riches of his grace in his kindness toward us through Christ Jesus."

Ephesians 2:5–7

Jesus didn't wait for us to be good enough or holy enough to die for. He knew that would never happen. He loved us even when we were sinners. Even when we were dead in sins, God "quickened" us—made us alive— together with Christ by His Holy Spirit. By His grace you are saved. God has raised us up together with Christ (if we've been buried, then we've also been raised); God has made us sit together in heavenly places in Christ Jesus. If He is the head and we are the body, then we are sitting with Him at the right hand of the Father. We have been made joint heirs with Christ, so whatever He has inherited we are joint heirs to as well. The Father is full of kindness toward His children. He is going to show us in the agesto come the exceeding riches of His grace. The things we are going to experience are above what we can even imagine.

"For we are his workmanship created in Christ Jesus unto good works, which God hath before ordained that we should walk in them."

Ephesians 2:10

God is the potter; we are the clay. Isaiah 64:8 says, "But now, O LORD, thou art our father; we are the clay, and thou our potter; and we all are the work of thy hand." We are his workmanship, and He is directing our steps. Ephesians 2:10 says, "Long ago, God ordained that we should walk in good works, as we are in Christ Jesus. As we abide in the vine which is Jesus, as we stay connected to him, we will bear much fruit." We will walk in those good works, for it will be a natural thing. We have a relationship with the Father, Son, and Holy Spirit. God's life will permeate our being. We are to realize His love for us as we meditate. We will be so loved that it can't help but flood through us onto others, thus bringing and bearing the good fruit. If we are disconnected to the vine, we will bear no fruit.

"But now in Christ Jesus ye who sometimes were far off are made nigh by the blood of Christ. For he is our peace who hath made both one, and hath broken down the middle wall of partition between us;"

Ephesians 2:13–14

When we were in the kingdom of darkness, we were so very far away from God, and our eyes were blinded; we were deceived. Because of Jesus and His death for us in our place, He has made us near to God by His precious and holy blood. He made peace for us with God. There used to be a wall in between us. We could not get to God because of our sin nature, so God came to us. Matthew 27:51 says, "And behold the veil of the temple was rent in twain from the top to the bottom…" God made this happen. The Spirit of God tore that veil. He did not want any more walls between Him and His children. He is a good Father who wants His kids by His side. Through the blood of Jesus, we have no more walls. We can come close in peace now.

"For through him we both have access by one Spirit unto the Father. Now therefore ye are no more strangers and foreigners, but fellow citizens with the saints, and of the household of God; And are built upon the foundation of the apostles and prophets, Jesus Christ himself being the chief corner stone; In whom all the building fitly framed together groweth unto an holy temple in the Lord:"

Ephesians 2:18–21

What a beautiful first statement. There is so much unity here: one Father, one Spirit—one Lord and one body. Through Jesus, we now have access; we have a way to the Father through the Spirit. There is no more distance, and we are no longer strangers. We belong to the family of God. We belong to His kingdom, and we are in His household as citizens and as a family. Without Him, we are all nothing. We all are built around Him into a perfect fit as we grow together into a holy temple in the Lord.

"In whom we have boldness and access with confidence by the faith of him."
Ephesians 3:12

In Christ, we have boldness now, for we stand in Him. In ourselves we are weak, but in Him, we have confidence through our faith in Him. The reason we have confidence is that we are secure in and sure of His work. We know He did enough. He shed enough blood. He took enough stripes on His back to pay for all of our sickness and disease. He went to the depths of hell as no one else would for us. Only He could do this, and He did enough. So we have boldness and access to God with confidence. Access means the right to approach and the ability and right to use.

"And be found in him, not having mine own righteousness, which is of the law, but that which is through the faith of Christ, the righteousness which is of God by faith: That I may know him, and the power of his resurrection, and the fellowship of his sufferings, being made conformable unto his death;"
Philippians 3:9–10

It is through faith in Christ that I have become the righteousness of God. Yes, we are the ones who believe, but even that faith was given to us by Jesus. So my faith and my righteousness come from Jesus that I may know Him. It is all about relationship; He is our friend, our Savior, our Shepherd, and our King. He is so much to us. He walks with us and gives us victory, even in the sufferings and persecutions that we experience in this life; we are experiencing some of what He experienced, even if only a taste. It brings us closer to Him; even in our pain we can fellowship with Him. We are conforming to His death.

"I can do all things through Christ which strengtheneth me."

Philippians 4:13

Alone, all I have are my own limited abilities and accomplishments, but when I am looking to these, it is very easy for me to become prideful. What are they compared to Christ's accomplishments? It is actually all right to see myself as weak and limited. For if I see myself as strong, I won't need Christ. Second Corinthians 12:9 makes clear that whenwe are weak, He is strong; His grace is sufficient for us. All that He did on the cross for us was—and is—enough. It is His work, and it is His grace. I can do some limited things by myself. But through Him there are no limits as to what I can do. I can do anything He leads me to do. I must be Spirit led in life, for any other way is a waste of time. He is the one who strengthens me; He is my ability and my wisdom.

"But my God shall supply all your need according to his riches in glory by Christ Jesus."

Philippians 4:19

The riches in glory by Christ Jesus far outweigh any vast riches on this earth. Part of the provision of the cross is that Jesus died for our poverty. Second Corinthians 8:9 says, "For ye know the grace of our Lord Jesus Christ, that, though he was rich, yet for your sakes he became poor, that ye through his poverty might be rich." He took on our poverty so that we could take His riches. It was a great exchange and in our favor. There is absolutely no need in heaven, for God does not have any need.

The needs are here on earth. And this verse says, "my God"—He is our God. He shall supply ALL your need. Not one need is left out. But there is a string attached: You must believe and trust Him,

"Giving thanks unto the Father, which hath made us meet to be partakers of the inheritance of the saints in light: Who hath delivered us from the power of darkness, and hath translated us into the kingdom of his dear Son: In whom we have redemption through his blood, even the forgiveness of sins:"

Colossians 1:12–14

Amplified:

"Giving thanks to the Father, who has qualified and made us fit to share the portion which is the inheritance of the saints (God's holy people) in the Light. [The Father] has delivered and drawn us to Himself out of the control and the dominion of darkness and has transferred us into the kingdom of the Son of His love in Whom we have our redemption through his blood, [which means] the forgiveness of our sins."

We have the Father to thank for this wonderful life. Give thanks to Him, for He has qualified and made us fit to be partakers of the inheritance of the saints in lights. We have an inheritance. There is so much to look forward to! We have all eternity to spend with each other and the Father, Jesus, and the Holy Spirit, not to mention all the saints that have gone before us. We are in the family of God! We are on the winning side—what have we to fear? We put too much focus on the devil, who has already lost. I want to show you a verse that speaks of Satan and how we will look at him in the end.

"I will ascend above the heights of the clouds; I will be like the most High. Yet thou shalt be brought down to hell, to the sides of the pit. They that see thee shall narrowly look upon thee, and consider thee, saying, Is this the man that made the earth to tremble, that did shake kingdoms; that made the world as a wilderness, and destroyed the cities thereof; that opened not the house of his prisoners?"

Isaiah 14:14–17

He has deceived too many, but we don't have to be deceived any longer. God has delivered us from the power of darkness and has transferred us into the kingdom of the Son of His love. We are in a new kingdom now, not just in the future. In the spirit, it is now. We should see it and use our imaginations to picture this that has already become. Look past your circumstances, Saint. See the light that has come. See His glory. His blood has brought us redemption. His blood has brought us forgiveness—even the forgiveness of our sins.

"For by him were all things created, that are in heaven, and that are in earth, visible and invisible, whether they be thrones, or dominions, or principalities, or powers: all things were created by him, and for him: And he is before all things, and by him all things consist. And he is the head of the body, the church: who is the beginning, the firstborn from the dead; that in all things he might have the preeminence. For it pleased the Father that in him should all fulness dwell: And, having made peace through the blood of his cross, by him to reconcile all things unto himself."

Colossians 1:16–20

Jesus is one with God. Jesus has always been. He always will be. John 1:1 says, "In the beginning was the Word, and the Word was with God, and the Word was God. The same was in the beginning with God. All things were made by him; and without him was not any thing made that was made." All things—all things—were created by Him, in heaven and in earth, the seen and the unseen, no matter what they are, from thrones, or dominions, or principalities, or powers. And all things were created for Him. Jesus is before all things, and it is by Him that they are sustained. Jesus Christ is the head of the body, which is the church. He is the firstborn from the dead; He was the first to be raised from the dead and be born again. He occupies the chief place.

Philippians 2:8–10 says, "He humbled himself, and became obedient unto death, even the death of the cross. Wherefore God also hath highly exalted him, and given him a name which is above every name: that at the name of Jesus every knee should bow…." This pleased the Father. Jesus is the one who humbled his own self, and God blessed and rewarded Him and brought Him to the highest place. It was right in the Father's eyes for all the fullness of the godhead to dwell in Christ. Jesus is the one who made peace for us through the blood of His cross. It is by Jesus that the Father reconciled you to Himself.

"To whom God would make known what is the riches of the glory of this mystery among the Gentiles; which is Christ in you, the hope of glory:"

Colossians 1:27

The promise of the Messiah came first to the Jews, but they did not receive Him. And so then He went to the Gentiles, which is everyone who is not a Jew, meaning you and me. What is this mystery that comes from the riches of His glory? The mystery is this: Christ in you. The verse before speaks that this mystery was hidden for ages and generations, even hidden from the angels and men. God is brilliant and full of all wisdom. He is the one who chose to have Christ in us, the hope of glory. We needed to have His Spirit living in us while we were on this earth. We couldn't make it on our own. With Christ in us, abiding in us, and we in Him, we will experience fruit growing to feed others. We will be energized by His Spirit even as we are praying with the wonderful gift He has given freely to us. He lives in us. We have His life-giving power in us, and this is forever and ever, amen.

"For in him dwelleth all the fullness of the Godhead bodily. And ye are complete in him which is the head of all principality and power:"

Colossians 2:9–10

This first phrase speaks of the Holy Trinity. The fullness of the Godhead is Father, Son, and Holy Spirit. This fullness dwells in Jesus bodily. And we are complete in Him, which means the Father, Son, and Holy Spirit live in us as well. We are complete. You can read this in John 14:23: "If a man love me, he will keep my words: and my Father will love him, and we will come unto him, and make our abode with him." We don't have to understand it but just receive it by grace. We are in His family, and He loves us and wants to include us in everything. He is the head of all principality and power. There is no power that is above Jesus.

"If ye then be risen with Christ, seek those things which are above, where Christ sitteth on the right hand of God. Set your affection on things above, not on things on the earth. For ye are dead, and your life is hid with Christ in God. When Christ, who is our life, shall appear, then shall ye also appear with him in glory."

Colossians 3:1–4

Think of how you are a new creation, a new breed. Old things are passed away. You're in a new kingdom; all things are made new. Come into this new kingdom, and find out about the new ways. They are higher, and there is freedom and grace beyond measure. You are dead from your old sin nature, and now your life is hidden with Christ in God. He sits at the right hand of God the Father, and it is right for you to seek those things, which are above where Christ sits, for you are a joint heir with Christ and you also sit in heavenly places. You should no longer set your heart on the things of this world. Once you realize how much you have in Christ, you will never want to go back to the old life; it will smell putrid and could never compare to the new life in Christ.

"I the LORD have called thee in righteousness, and will hold thine hand, and will keep thee, and give thee for a covenant of the people, for a light of the Gentiles; To open the blind eyes, to bring out the prisoners from the prison, and them that sit in darkness out of the prison house."

Isaiah 42:6–7

This is an Old Testament verse prophetic of the things to come in the New Testament. Now we can look back and see what has become because of Jesus. Here God is speaking to Jesus: "I have called thee in righteousness, and will hold your hand, and will keep you, I will give you for a covenant of the people, for a light of the Gentiles. To open the blind eyes, to bring out the prisoners from the prison, and them that sit in darkness out of the prison house." And Jesus did just that. He came as a light to us, the Gentiles. He came to make a New Covenant with us that would never end. He made the covenant for us with God. He has opened our eyes and brought out the prisoners, those that sat in darkness, from the prison.

"And the grace of our Lord was exceeding abundant with faith and love which is in Christ Jesus."

Timothy 1:14

Faith and love are in Jesus, and yet they are inside of us as well because Jesus is living in us. This is due to the fact that His grace is exceedingly abundant for us. And in His grace is all that we need in this life and into the next life eternal. Through the cross, He provided all of His never-ending, exceeding grace. We are speaking of not just any love but the God kind of love, which is agape love and unconditional. He loves us just because. And it's not just any faith. It's the God kind of faith. He supplied everything for us.

"Who hath saved us, and called us with an holy calling, not according to our works, but according to his own purpose and grace, which was given us in Christ Jesus before the world began."

Timothy 1:9

Way before the world began God had called us with a holy calling according to His own purpose and grace. This free grace was given by Jesus. He didn't only save us; He could have just done that, and that would have been wonderful in itself, but He gave us so much. God has done things on our behalf because of His love and mercy— because of His grace— not because of our works. We do good works not to earn our way but because we love God. We are not saved by our works. We are saved by His works.

"Thou therefore, my son, be strong in the grace that is in Christ Jesus."

2 Timothy 2:1

We are His children, and He loves and corrects us in love as His children. He provided an abundance of grace through His Son Jesus. Don't be strong in your own strength or in your works and accomplishments. Be strong in His grace. If you are strong in your own works, you will not be strong in His grace.

"It is a faithful saying: For if we be dead with him, we shall also live with him:"

2 Timothy 2:11

Both should be strong revelations in our hearts. How can you live in Christ unless you have first died within? And if you are dead in Christ, shouldn't you also be alive with Him? If you are in Christ, then you should also consider yourself to be dead to the old man, the sin nature, and your old spirit man—and also even more consider yourself alive in Jesus. Don't go back and live in the past, for your life is now hid in Christ Jesus. Look ahead to the future. It is bright, not gloomy. It is full of hope and glorious, supernatural wonders.

"But after that the kindness and love of God our Saviour toward man appeared, Not by works of righteousness which we have done, but according to his mercy he saved us, by the washing of regeneration, and renewing of the Holy Ghost; Which he shed on us abundantly through Jesus Christ our Saviour; That being justified by his grace, we should be made heirs according to the hope of eternal life."

Titus 3:4–7

The previous verse speaks of how we were disobedient and evil before Jesus appeared with the love of God for us all. He didn't save us because we were good, nor for our acts of righteousness, but because of His mercy. We became born again and regenerated in Him by the renewing of the Holy Spirit. He generously gave us the gift of the Holy Spirit. He justified us by His grace, so now we are as if we never sinned. He made us heirs with Him according to the hope of eternal life.

"That the communication of thy faith may become effectual by the acknowledging of every good thing which is in you in Christ Jesus."

Philemon 1:6

Beautiful, good things are in Christ and Christ is in us, which means so many wonderful things have been given to us! It is very possible for you and me to have effectual communication as Paul and even Peter did in the book of Acts after the cross of Jesus. People knew that they had been with Jesus. They had the Spirit of God and the mind of Christ. We do too, but we need knowledge of His Word. We need to find out what we have in Christ so that we can use it.

"Neither by the blood of goats and calves, but by his own blood he entered in once into the holy place, having obtained eternal redemption for us."

Hebrews 9:12

In the Old Testament, the high priest would offer up the blood of goats and calves for people's sins. Once a year he would offer up a lamb without spot or wrinkle for the sins of his people, but this would only cover them for a year. They were used to living this way, from year to year with animal sacrifices. We no longer live this way. In the New Covenant, we live under a new and permanent way—not by the blood of animals. It's a supernatural God way. Jesus entered one time into the holy place in heaven and shed His blood as an offering for us. Revelation 1:5 speaks of how He washed us from our sins in His own body.

By this He obtained eternal redemption for us—the forgiveness of your sins past, present, and future, are covered under this eternal redemption. Once you realize this, you will be set free from a sin-conscious, guilt-ridden attitude.

"Now the God of peace, that brought again from the dead our Lord Jesus, that great shepherd of the sheep, through the blood of the everlasting covenant, make you perfect in every good work to do his will, working in you that which is well pleasing in his sight, through Jesus Christ; to whom be glory for ever and ever. Amen."

Hebrews 13:20–21

God is love, but he is also Jehovah Shalom, which means peace. He is the one who raised Jesus from the dead. He is our great Shepherd, and we are His sheep. Through the blood of Jesus, God made a New Covenant on our behalf, an everlasting one. It is through this Covenant that He makes us perfect in every good work in order to do His will. He is always working in us that which is well pleasing to His sight. He is always looking out for your welfare to bless you and for you to be a blessing. And this is all through Christ, to whom be glory forever and ever. Amen.

"But ye are a chosen generation, a royal priesthood, an holy nation, a peculiar people; that ye should shew forth the praises of him who hath called you out of darkness into his marvelous light;"

1 Peter 2:9

You were chosen by God. You are in a different kingdom. On this earth, it is backwards—people are important according to how much fame or money they have. In God's kingdom, everyone is important.

Every child of God is valued and accepted in the beloved. You are a royal priesthood, a holy nation. You are different than the world. We are deeply loved; it is all because of Jesus that we have these benefits. We should not be silent or hidden. We should shine! We should give Him glory! We should shew forth to all the praises of God! He has been generous to us! He has called us out of darkness and into His marvelous light!

"Now unto him that is able to keep you from falling, and to present you faultless before the presence of his glory with exceeding joy, to the only wise God our Saviour, be glory and majesty, dominion and power for ever and ever. Amen."

Jude 1:24

Trust Jesus. Lean on Him and believe Him. He is the one who has traveled so far for you and me. He is able to keep you from falling as you trust Him and His Word. He is able to sustain you. He is able to present you faultless to His Father because you will be faultless and holy in Him. He is going to present you with an exceeding joy before the presence of His glory to the only wise God, our Savior, be glory and majesty, dominion forever and ever. Amen.

"Unto him that loved us, and washed us from our sins in his own blood, and hath made us kings and priests unto God and his Father; to him be glory and dominion for ever and ever. Amen."

Revelation 1:5–6

Jesus loves us. It was for love that He died for us. He washed our sins from our whole life in His own blood. He made the sacrifice. He is the champion of our souls. He didn't wash our sins in just any blood from an animal, or even a pure and clean animal, as in the Old Testament. That would have lasted only a year, like it did in the Old Testament when the priests would offer up animals to cover the sins of the people. He washed our sins in His very own blood. This demonstrates how deep His love runs. He was willing to give His own life for you. He could have left it at that, but He went further. He is the one who made you a king and a priest unto God His Father. Most people cannot fathom this or have never even heard of it. What does a king do? He decrees orders. So you and I were meant to speak and decree His Word and to decree life. As for a priest, they offer up prayers and worship unto God. We offer up our lives as a living sacrifice unto God as in Romans 12:2.

Meditations 5 –
I Am Healed

This section will outline what it means to be healed by Jesus. What He did for us on the cross is more than the forgiveness of sins. We will be meditating on scriptures that speak of the healing that Christ died to purchase for us.

"But his delight is in the law of the LORD; and in his law doth he meditate day and night. And he shall be like a tree planted by the rivers of water, that bringeth forth his fruit in his season; his leaf also shall not wither; and whatsoever he doeth shall prosper."

Psalm 1:2–3

"My son, attend to my words; incline thine ear unto my sayings. Let them not depart from thine eyes; keep them in the midst of thine heart. For they are life unto those that find them, and health to all their flesh."

Proverbs 4:20–22

"I beseech you therefore, brethren, by the mercies of God, that ye present your bodies a living sacrifice, holy, acceptable unto God, which is your reasonable service. And be not conformed to this world: but be ye transformed by the renewing of your mind, that ye may prove what is that good, and acceptable, and perfect, will of God."

Romans 12:1–2

It is not a waste of time to put your thoughts and your mind on God's Word—quite the opposite. You will be doing well for yourself: your body, your mind, and your future. It is rather a waste of time to worry and to only see and think on the problem. To dwell on the hopeless circumstances can only bring death.

You can choose to make a new habit. When you keep your thoughts on His Word, eventually it will come out of your mouth and you will reap the benefits from it. You will have more peace, better health, and many more positive thoughts full of life. This will happen as you give yourself to thinking on the Scriptures. But don't take my word for it—put it to the test for yourself! I would love to lead you in beginning to meditate on these things.

Many of you, I believe, will receive your healing as you allow these scriptures to come alive to you and as you imagine them to be real in your heart. Just as you read about these people long ago receiving their healing, you, too, will experience your own healing from Jesus of Nazareth. I'm excited for you.

Let's begin:

"So Abraham prayed unto God: and God healed Abimelech, and his wife, and his maidservants; and they bare children."

Genesis 20:17

This tells us that God heard Abraham's prayers and that He heard the prayers Abraham prayed for someone else—not just someone else but his wife and their maidservants as well. God cares for all, and He healed the barrenness. Servants are people too, and God cared for their well-being as much as those they answered to.

"For thou hast delivered my soul from death, mine eyes from tears, and my feet from falling. I will walk before the LORD in the land of the living."

Psalm 116:8–9

If you think about this scripture in the New Testament, you could look at this verse as provision for spirit, soul, and body. Jesus has delivered your soul from death by taking your place so that you don't have to die. He alone delivered your eyes from tears, for Isaiah 53:4 states, "He bore my griefs and carried my sorrows." You don't have to live in sadness. You can give it to Him and take His peace and His joy. And if you trust in Him, He will keep your feet from falling, which is speaking of your body. Through His death you have been given life. You can make the choice to take it and walk in it.

"Behold, I will bring it health and cure, and I will cure them, and will reveal unto them the abundance of peace and truth.

Jeremiah 33:6

The Lord wants to be our source for all things. He loves to care for us. It is not a chore. He does not see us as an obligation. You can suffer with symptoms of sickness for years if you want to or receive His provision by faith— receive His healing.

"Trust in the LORD with all thine heart; and lean not unto thine own understanding. In all thy ways acknowledge him, and he shall direct thy paths. Be not wise in thine own eyes: fear the LORD, and depart from evil. It shall be health to thy navel, and marrow to thy bones."

Proverbs 3:5–8

Few people trust God. Most people trust themselves, make their own plans, and decide for themselves what to do and when to do it. Can they see up ahead? No. Only God knows what's up ahead. We would do well to trust Him with all of our hearts and put all of our trust in Him. Not only should we not trust ourselves but we shouldn't even lean that way. In all of your ways, in every way, acknowledge Him. Think about Him and His wisdom. As youdo, He shall direct your path. And as you do, it will even be "health to your navel and marrow to your bones."

"Who his own self bare our sins in his own body on the tree, that we, being dead to sins, should live unto righteousness: by whose stripes ye were healed."

1 Peter 2:24

Jesus didn't have someone do it for Him. He did it Himself. He willingly bore the whole world's sin in His own body on the tree. He who never knew sin became sin for us. Sin is ugly, and sin is death. Can you imagine this? Just think of the sin of one person. Think of their whole life. Now multiply that until you have every single man, woman, and child in the whole world. There is an estimated seven billion people on this earth today. That is a heavy, heavy weight on one person. It was all put on Jesus—not only the sin but the sickness of the whole world as well. Isaiah 52:14 states that his visage (how he looked) was marred more than that of any man and his form more than the sons of men.

The next phrase in 1 Peter 2:24 says that we are dead to sins and should live unto righteousness. We died with Him, for He took our place, took our sins, and took our sicknesses and then gave us His righteousness. He paid for us to live unto righteousness. "By whose stripes ye were healed." The stripes were the lashes on the back of Jesus. He did the work on the cross. We go free from sickness and sin, but He did the work. We get the benefit.

"And great multitudes came unto him, having with them those that were lame, blind, dumb, maimed, and many others, and cast them down at Jesus'

feet; and he healed them: Insomuch that the multitude wondered, when they saw the dumb to speak, the maimed to be whole, the lame to walk, and the blind to see: and they glorified the God of Israel."

Matthew 15:30–31

If we can get this picture, what an amazing scene it must have been. This doesn't say a few people or a crowd came but a great multitude. Once people saw miracles, they came by the droves. They were desperate. Word traveled. In many places in the gospels it says that his fame traveled. He didn't heal and preach for the fame though. He didn't have wrong motives. His motives were of pure love and compassion. Families were bringing their relatives and friends who were sick and had all kinds of different diseases. And Jesus healed them all.

"And withersoever he entered, into villages, or cities, or country, they laid the sick in the streets, and besought him that they might touch if it were but the border of his garment: and as many as touched him were made whole."

Mark 6:56

He was famous! That's not what His motive was, but that's what human nature does. When someone does wonders or the unusual, the word gets around, and everyone comes out of the woodwork to see. It says "withersoever," which means wherever He went. As soon as He even entered a village or a city or a country, they came. The word went out fast! He could not be alone; they followed Him everywhere! It sounds like a circus! Picture them laying the sick in the streets, making sure He would see them as He came into town. They didn't care what it looked like; they were determined to get their healing. They sought Him that they might touch even the border of His garment. As many as touched Him were made whole. It does not say they were half healed but that they were made WHOLE.

"And he arose out of the synagogue, and entered into Simon's house. And Simon's wife's mother was taken with a great fever; and they besought him for her. And he stood over her, and rebuked the fever; and it left her: and immediately she arose and ministered unto them."

Luke 4:38–39

Jesus was always teaching in the synagogue. You can picture Him with the wisdom of God flowing out of His mouth. He arose and came into Simon's house, where his mother-in-law had a high fever. They had gone to get Jesus. It doesn't say that He touched her;it says He stood over her. All He had to do was rebuke the fever, which means He spoke to the fever. He always spoke with authority. It left her. She didn't just recuperate and rest for a few days. Wow—it says she got up immediately and served them! So get this picture: Not only did the high fever leave but strength also came into her body right away. God is good

"Now when the sun was setting, all they that had any sick with divers diseases brought them unto him; and he laid his hands on every one of them, and healedthem. And devils also came out of many, crying out, and saying, Thou art Christ the Son of God. And he rebuking them suffered them not to speak: for they knew that he was Christ.

Luke 4:40–41

I love this verse and how it describes the sun setting. There are a lot of people in the world, and the strength that Jesus had to minister to so many people is astounding. "All they that had any sick" brought them unto Him. In a town or village, who knows how many this could be. But Jesus never stopped being compassionate; His mercy never ended, and so He laid hands on every one of them and healed them. This is where it was happening, which means those that were not sick were probably there to watch and see what was going on. Demons were coming out and screaming as they left, but He rebuked and commanded them not to speak. Even the demons knew who He was. The day of Pentecost had not come yet. (That's the day in the first few chapters in the book of Acts when Jesus said to the disciples to go and wait for the power to come to them.) This verse was before that day, yet they were able to cure diseases and cast out devils. They did this only because Jesus had given them power and authority to do so. And He sent them to preach the kingdom of God two by two. They were in training; they must have been so excited. Up until then, only Jesus had done all the miracles, but now it was multiplying and growing. This is how the kingdom of God works. God the Father is all about growing, building, and blessing. He doesn't tear down people. The works of God are to build people up.

"Then he called his twelve disciples together, and gave them power and authority over all devils, and to cure diseases. And he sent them to preach the kingdom of God, and to heal the sick."

Luke 9:1–2

God gave Jesus power. And Jesus gave the disciples power—power and authority over ALL devils, power and authority to cure diseases. He sent them to preach but not to preach the law—to preach the kingdom of God. God didn't send Jesus to condemn but to save, to heal, and to show mercy. There was enough judgment already in the world. Mercy was needed, and mercy had come just in time. He sent them to heal the sick. What an exciting day that must have been for them. They also had to overcome any fear or intimidation. A new day had dawned.

"Now when he came nigh to the gate of the city, behold, there was a dead man carried out, the only son of his mother, and she was a widow: and much people of the city was with her. And when the Lord saw her, he had compassion on her, and said unto her, Weep not. And he came and touched the bier: and they that bare him stood still. And he said, Young man, I say unto thee, Arise. And he that was dead sat up, and began to speak. And he delivered him to his mother.

Luke 7:12–1

5

The gate of the city is the entry to or exit from a people's way of life. Through this particular gate, there came a funeral procession of a woman who had lost her husband already and had just experienced the loss of her only son. The scripture says there were "much" people with her, but that never seemed to phase Jesus. He was focused on helping and ministering to people; He was focused on destroying the works of the devil (1 John 3:8). He was near the gate and saw as they were carrying this bier of the son out of the city. He saw her, and He must have seen deep into her heart, which was full of sorrow; He had compassion on her. He got close enough to her to speak and have her hear Him say, "Weep not." I'm sure she knew who He was; there are scriptures that speak of how His fame was spread abroad because of all the miracles that He did. I'm betting her eyes, though full of tears, were fixed on Him even as He walked and came closer and closer. What was in their minds? It says, "They that bare him stood still." I'll bet you could hear a pin drop. What was He going to do next? Jesus dared to speak to the dead son. Who would talk to a dead person? You might talk to your loved one who is passed laying in the coffin. You might say goodbye, but you surely don't expect them to talk back. Jesus did though. He said, "Young man, I say unto thee, arise." They must have been riveted. The boy sat up and talked. I wish I could have been there to see their faces, to see her face. She must have screamed and cried for joy! Jesus delivered him to her. She had her only son back again—alive!

"And a certain man was there, which had an infirmity thirty and eight years. When Jesus saw him lie, and knew that he had been now a long time in that case, he saith unto him, Wilt thou be made whole? The impotent man answered him, Sir, I have no man, when the water is troubled, to put me into the pool: but while I am coming, another steppeth down before me. Jesus saith unto him, Rise, take up thy bed, and walk.' And immediately the man was made whole, and took up his bed, and walked..."

John 5:5–9

To have an infirmity for thirty-eight years is a lifetime. It's the same as someone being in prison for forty years—it becomes all you know. It shapes the picture of how you see yourself. Proverbs 23:7 says, "As he thinketh in his heart, so is he." You have this picture ingrained in your mind of how you see yourself, and you have looked at it so long, you believe it is who you are. But Jesus dared to ask the man by the pool, "Will you be made whole?" It was a question, and He was waiting for the man to give the answer. Instead, the man gave an excuse. He blamed his problem on others. But Jesus didn't let it go. He put the responsibility on him—in fact, it was a challenge or even a command. "Rise, take up thy bed, and walk." This was his day. The scripture says, "Immediately the man was made whole, and took up his bed, and walked." We must see our healing in our minds. We must make some steps to action. He is the healer, but we choose to be healed and put some action to it every day.

"He healeth the broken in heart, and bindeth up their wounds."

Psalm 147:3

He heals our bodies, but He is also a master at healing our hearts. He can heal every part of us because He made us. He is our creator. He can heal our broken hearts. He binds up our wounds; the Hebrew meaning is to wrap firmly. "Wounds" refers to sorrow or pain. Allow Him to bandage your pain. Come to Him and receive healing for your heart, for the past. Don't live in the past any longer. Give it to Jesus.

"But unto you that fear my name shall the Sun of righteousness arise with healing in his wings; and ye shall go forth, and grow up as calves of the stall."

Malachi 4:2

To fear His name is to revere and honor Him, to have a holy fear of God, for He is awesome and powerful. To fear Him is to believe Him, and to believe in Him is to believe in His Son.

One would think that the "sun of righteousness" is a misprint, but I don't believe so. Could it be that what was trying to be said is that Jesus is so bright in His glory that He is as the sun? Righteousness comes from Him, and we are righteous in Him. He has risen in power and glory, and He has risen with healing in His wings. Healing that would fly to us— this is such a beautiful word picture; just see and imagine it. He touches us, and we receive what He has paid for. It causes us to be strong and go forth.

"And when Jesus departed thence, two blind men followed him, crying, and saying, Thou son of David, have mercy on us. And when he was come into the house, the blind men came to him: and Jesus saith unto them, Believe ye that I am able to do this? They said unto him, Yea, Lord. Then touched he their eyes, saying, According to your faith be it unto you. And their eyes were opened..."

Matthew 9:27–30

It had to have taken quite an effort for two blind men to stumble and follow Jesus as He left. They were determined and didn't care if anyone saw them or heard them. They cried out. They only knew that

Jesus had something they needed. They didn't think of what was proper when they cried out, "Thou son of David, have mercy on us." It says they came to Him, and Jesus said to them, "Believe ye that I am able to do this?" They said yes. He put His hand on their eyes, "According to your faith, be it unto you," and their eyes were opened. This phrase, "according to your faith," is speaking about your expectation. What were they expecting? If one of them would have said, "Well, if you could just make my body stronger so I can get around better even though I am blind," that may have been all he received, according to his faith. The Lord will meet you where you are.

"And great multitudes followed him; and he healed them there."

Matthew 19:

This is surely a word picture. It doesn't say a few people or even a multitude, but it says a great multitude. A multitude can be a throng or a company of people, and this was a great one.

Because of all the miracles, healings, and deliverances that Jesus did, word had spread quickly. He was famous whether He wanted to be or not. This is how the human nature can be; they follow the latest news and such whether it's correct or not. This doesn't mean it's the right thing to do; it's just how most people are. Some who are famous love it. Others hate crowds following them, but Jesus was always compassionate because He loved them. He was there to heal them.

"How God anointed Jesus of Nazareth with the Holy Ghost and with power: who went about doing good, and healing all that were oppressed of the devil; for God was with him."

Acts 10:38

God the Father is the one who anointed Jesus; He anointed Him with the Holy Ghost and with power. All the works that Jesus did came from the Father. He was sent by the Father, and He spoke what the Father spoke. This means that whatever Jesus did, whatever we read that He did, He did because of the Father. He told His disciples that if you've seen me, you've seen the Father. We get a good picture of what the Father is like by looking at Jesus. Jesus went around doing good. The Father is good. Jesus didn't strike people with disease. God doesn't strike people with disease. He always wants to heal. He always is full of power. He will never change, and His power will never end.

"My son, forget not my law; but let thine heart keep my commandments; For length of days, and long life, and peace, shall they add to thee."

Proverbs 3:1–2

Romans 5:1 says, "Therefore being justified by faith, we have peace with God through our Lord Jesus Christ." In the Old Testament, they followed the Law and the Ten Commandments. But Jesus came to fulfill the Law because we could not. Now the new commandment is to love. John 13:34 says, "A new commandment I give unto you, That ye love one another; as I have loved you, that ye also love one another." In the Old Testament, if you remembered and kept the Law, it would mean long life, length of days, and peace. Now, in the New Testament, as we love and renew our minds on His Word, keeping His Word in our hearts and making it first place in our lives, we see length of days, long life, and peace. These will be added to us. This is a promise we can receive in our lives.

"And Jesus went about all Galilee, teaching in their synagogues, and preaching the gospel of the kingdom, and healing all manner of sickness and all manner of disease among the people. And his fame went throughout Syria: and they brought unto him all sick people that were taken with divers diseases and torments, and those which were possessed with devils, and those which were lunatic, and those that had the palsy; and he healed them."

Matthew 4:23–24

Jesus wasn't afraid of anything or anyone, anywhere. He went all about Galilee, teaching right in the Jewish synagogues. He preached the gospel and was not intimidated at all. The gospel was the good news, and He not only preached it but He did it. He healed all manner of sickness and disease. His fame continued to spread. People continued to bring the sick and tormented to Him, the possessed and the lunatic, the palsy; He healed them. This was His purpose. However, no matter what good He had done, people came against him. But His mercy triumphed over judgment.

"My son, attend to my words; incline thine ear unto my sayings. Let them not depart from thine eyes; keep them in the midst of thine heart. For they are life unto those that find them, and health to all their flesh."

Proverbs 4:20–23

This gives us a more defined way of how to meditate. You are His child; this is His instruction to you for success and health. Attend to His words. Bend your ear to hear His sayings. You come and bend your ear; you make the effort. You have to go after it. You are to let them not leave your eyes. You are either looking at the world or looking at God's Word. Keep His words in the midst of your heart. They are life unto those that find them. Go and look after it; it will be life to you. His Word is full of life, and His words are health to all your flesh, to every bit of your flesh, inside and out.

"For this purpose the Son of God was manifested, that he might destroy the works of the devil."

1 John 3:8

This was His purpose. His showing and life on Earth had a purpose: not to judge or to condemn, not to strike you out but to strike out Satan, to destroy and annihilate the evil works of the enemy. God hates evil, not the sinner; He loves the sinner, but He hates sickness that kills, destruction that hurts, sorrow and pain that break your heart. God is for you, not against you. Get it straight; Satan hates and destroys. Satan is bad; God is good.

"And they bring a blind man unto him, and besought him to touch him. And he took the blind man by the hand, and led him out of the town; and when he had spit on his eyes, and put his hands upon him, he asked him if he saw ought. And he looked up, and said, I see men as trees, walking. After that he put his hands again upon his eyes, and made him look up: and he was restored, and saw every man clearly."

Mark 8:22–25

God will ask us to do different things sometimes to receive our healing because each person is unique. It is our obedience that is important. The blind man let Him spit on his eyes. The blind man let Him put His hand upon him and lead him out of town. They must have had a bit of a walk in order to go out of town. Did they talk, and what did they talk about? Could Jesus have asked him questions? It doesn't say if they talked, but after He laid hands on him, He asked if he could see. He saw the shapes of men like trees. It's okay to lay your hands on someone again as you are praying. You are speaking to their body. You are commanding their body to obey and respond to the Word of God. He laid His hands again, and the blind man was restored and saw every man clearly. Only God could do this in a matter of minutes.

"Insomuch that they brought forth the sick into the streets, and laid them on beds and couches, that at the least the shadow of Peter passing by might overshadow some of them. There came also a multitude out of the cities round about unto Jerusalem, bringing sick folks, and them which were vexed with unclean spirits: and they were healed every one."

Acts 5:15–16

Can you picture this? It must have looked like a parade. It is amazing to think that even the shadow of the apostle Peter brought healing. Jesus is the one who provided the healing then and now. And if the Spirit of God dwells inside a person, that power is in there to bring healing to yourself and to others. That is the same power that raised Christ from the dead. Picture Peter walking by all those sick folks and those vexed with unclean spirits. They were all healed. Close your eyes and dare to picture yourself in the same spot as Peter.

You are aware of God's presence and power inside of you. You are willing to lay hands on the sick, and when you touch them, they are healed. You are the vessel, and it is His power. As you allow Him to use you and believe it, wonderful things can take place.

"I call heaven and earth to record this day against you, that I have set before you life and death, blessing and cursing: therefore choose life, that both thou and thy seed may live:"

Deuteronomy 30:19

God created life. He is all about life and blessing. God is about growing and building. Here He gives you a question, but He also gives you the answer. He doesn't want you to miss it. "Choose Life!"—that both you and your children may live. We have a choice! Choose life.

"There was a man whose right hand was withered. And the scribes and Pharisees watched him, whether he would heal on the sabbath day; that they might find an accusation against him. But he knew their thoughts, and said to the man which had the withered hand, Rise up, and stand forth in the midst. And he arose and stood forth. Then said Jesus unto them, I will ask you one thing; Is it lawful on the sabbath days to do good, or to do evil? to save life, or to destroy it? And looking round about upon them all, he said unto the man, Stretch forth thy hand. And he did so: and his hand was restored whole as the other."

Luke 6:6–10

Jesus went around doing good and healing people. So if this man was in His presence, it would have been like a magnet to the eyes of Jesus. He spotted sickness and disease from far away. He could sense it. There are guard dogs that the police use to smell drugs and such, and they are trained for this job. Jesus came to destroy the works of the enemy, so He was focused to see it. The scribes and Pharisees watched Him. They knew He would do something; they were after Him. But He was ahead of them already; He knew what they were planning.

God loves to show off by doing merciful acts. Jesus saw the man, and He saw the scribes. His love was so bold. He said to the man, "Rise up, and stand forth in the midst." He asked him to stand up and stand right in the middle of the crowd, front and center; He did not want the critical scribes and Pharisees to miss one detail of this show, this act of God. He asked them the questions. Then Jesus looked all around, making sure that He had their eyes on this man. He said, "Stretch forth thy hand." His hand was restored as whole as the other right in front of everyone. Praise be to God Almighty!

"And the people with one accord gave heed unto those things which Philip spake, hearing and seeing the miracles which he did. For unclean spirits, crying with loud voice, came out of many that were possessed with them: and many taken with palsies, and that were lame, were healed."

Acts 8:6–7

People gave heed because Philip spoke with authority. He had the Spirit of God. He knew who he was in Christ. People heard of the miracles God did through him, and they saw him move in miracles. Jesus told His disciples that they would do even greater works, for he was going to the Father. This goes for us as well. If the disciples did it, we can do it. Picture yourself in the place of Philip, being bold, taking your authority in Christ. Picture yourself healing those that are lame and casting out demons. They are not afraid of you alone but of Christ in you. And when you know your authority in Christ, they will cry with a loud voice and be afraid.

"Then went he down, and dipped himself seven times in Jordan, according to the saying of the man of God: and his flesh came again like unto the flesh of a little child, and he was clean."

2 Kings 5:14

The things that God asks us to do in order to receive our healing can be so different and unique to each individual. It's because He knows the heart of each individual. He loves us and wants us healed even more than we do. Thank God that He isn't a robot and that He doesn't treat us like robots, having us do the same prayer for every person.

This man dipped himself seven times in the Jordan; he did exactly what the man of God said. He was obedient, and God blesses obedience. Can you imagine his flesh turning into like that of a baby? How old was this man? When you read this chapter, this man had leprosy. His skin was damaged and diseased and being eaten away. With each dip into the water, could his healing have been taking place? Could people see it? Either way, he ended up with brand new flesh like a little baby. His end result was that he was clean.

"He sent his word, and healed them, and delivered them from their destructions. Oh that men would praise the LORD for his goodness, and for his wonderful works to the children of men!"

Psalm 107:20–21

He sent His word, which was Jesus. This is past tense. Each one of these verbs is past tense: sent, healed, and delivered from their destructions. Think about how many things can fit under destructions—accidents, bad habits, drug abuse, child abuse. Jesus paid the price for it all. He took the destruction on the cross. He paid for your sicknesses and for your destructions because He is a good God. And these are all part of His wonderful works.

Praise Him!

"And he said unto them, Go ye into all the world, and preach the gospel to every creature. He that believeth and is baptized shall be saved; but he that believeth not shall be damned. And these signs shall follow them that believe; In my name shall they cast out devils; they shall speak with new tongues; They shall take up serpents; and if they drink any deadly thing, it shall not hurt them; they shall lay hands on the sick, and they shall recover."

Mark 16:15–18

Jesus was telling the disciples this information. He was about to go to heaven, and these were some of His last words. His charge to them was "Go." He didn't say stay. He told them to go into all the world and preach the gospel to everyone. Everyone needs to hear the gospel. He told them that these signs would follow them that believe. Each one of these signs is supernatural, and in order to move in them, the person must believe in Jesus. If you are saved, you are eligible to move in this.

"The thief cometh not, but for to steal, and to kill, and to destroy: I am come that they might have life, and that they might have it more abundantly."

John 10:10

A thief does not come unless there might be something good to steal. He knows that Jesus brought life, but he doesn't want you to find it. If he can keep you away from the Word of God, he can keep you weak and unarmed. If you are unarmed, he will move right in and bring all kinds of destruction. He is even entertained by it. He hates God and anyone that God loves. He is the root of all destruction and evil. He brings destruction and then blames it on someone else. So many people in this world are walking in bitterness today from blaming God for the many years of hurt and destruction in their past because of Satan's lies. Don't fall for it.

Satan will get his in the end. He will be thrown into the lake of fire to be tormented day and night forever and ever (Rev. 20:10). God the Father, who is only good, will wipe away all tears from the eyes of His children, and there shall be no more death, neither sorrow, nor crying, nor pain (Rev. 21:4). Jesus said, "I am come that they might have life." He paid dearly for us to have it. Some will partake of it, and some won't. Some will go so far as to receive His abundant life! That would be me! And let it be you too!

"Wherefore lift up the hands which hang down, and the feeble knees; 13 And make straight paths for your feet, lest that which is lame be turned out of the way; but let it rather be healed."

Hebrews 12:12–13

To me, this says to stop feeling sorry for yourself. There is no need for that! Jesus paid the price already; He paved the way for health. Pick up your hands and praise and thank Him! See yourself the way He sees you—well and whole. Push past what you are feeling, and be determined to get a picture of wholeness. Keep coming back to that picture. See yourself as strong and vibrant.

"And when he thus had spoken, he cried with a loud voice, Lazarus, come forth. And he that was dead came forth, bound hand and foot with graveclothes: and his face was bound about with a napkin. Jesus saith unto them, Loose him, and let him go."

John 11:43–44

I encourage you to go to this chapter in your Bible and read the whole story to get all the details. It is very moving to picture in its entirety. In this particular account, it says Jesus cried with a loud voice. He called the name of Lazarus. Whoever was present was definitely spellbound and shaking, to say the least. Did they doubt? Did they think He was crazy to do such a thing? I don't know. But Lazarus obeyed, even all wrapped up from head to toe as he was. Jesus told them to loose him and let him go. He wouldn't need those cloths of death anymore, for he was alive! You can bet there was screaming and crying and every other kind of emotion. God was pleased to see the works of the devil destroyed. The sisters of Lazarus were pleased to see their brother. Jesus loved them, and He also was pleased to obey

His Father. Nothing is impossible with God. Life comes from the Father! Death comes from Satan.

"The tongue of the wise is health."

Proverbs 12:18

If you are wise, you will speak health and speak life. The very fact that this person is speaking health says that they are thinking health for the tongue is one of the last steps of the meditation process. Your words are the fruit of what is in your heart. First the imagination, then the thoughts are built, then the seeds are planted in your heart. A root is built, and the tree grows. Finally, the fruit comes out of the mouth, and then the action takes place. If you are wise to begin with, you will dwell on thoughts of healing, not fear and sickness.

"Pleasant words are as an honeycomb, sweet to the soul, and healthy to the bones."

Proverbs 16:24

Speak words of life. Don't speak doom and gloom. Think words of thankfulness and gratefulness. Count your blessings. Think on the good things like the scripture in Philippians 4:8: "Whatsoever things are of good report; if there be any virtue, and if there be any praise, think on these things." Think of the times that people spoke words that were cruel to you. You don't forget those times. You can go way back to when you were a child, and you have those memories. These can have an effect on you and even your body. So if that's so, it can go the opposite way as well. This verse says that pleasant words are healthy to your bones. That means that the words of our mouth are that important! They affect the very bones of your body, your very core.

"And, behold, a woman, which was diseased with an issue of blood twelve years, came behind him, and touched the hem of his garment: For she said within herself, If I may but touch his garment, I shall be whole. But Jesus turned him about, and when he saw her, he said, Daughter, be of good comfort; thy faith hath made thee whole. And the woman was made whole from that hour."

Matthew 9:20–22

When a woman had any problem with an issue of blood, she was considered unclean and needed to be separate from people, somewhat like the lepers stayed to themselves. But this woman was desperate and took the risk of being found out. She had to have thought out a plan. She must have even pictured how it could all possibly work out. For it says, "She said within herself, if I may but touch his garment, I shall be whole."

Maybe she figured since she was unclean, she wouldn't be able to speak to Him, but if she could sneak through the crowd and just touch Him that would be enough. She was expecting it. She came, and she did as she had planned. Jesus turned around and felt the power leave Him. He saw her, and maybe she was frightened that she was caught, but He had too much compassion to be angry. "Daughter, be of good comfort; thy faith has made you whole." Others would have shouted obscenities at her; she was used to that. But Jesus was gentle. And she was made completely whole from that hour.

"Bless the LORD, O my soul, and forget not all his benefits. Who forgiveth all thine iniquities; who healeth all thy diseases; who redeemeth thy life from destruction."

Psalm 103:2–4

We have no need for weeping. We have no need for complaining and whining. We should have experienced much tragedy and pain in your life, you can still thank Him for all the spiritual blessings. If you know Jesus, you have eternal life. And when you get to heaven, you have a mansion waiting in glory and a strong, healthy young body. You can have that even now in this life, but you must learn how to receive by faith, how to speak to your body. Learn to see yourself as God does.

"A merry heart doeth good like a medicine; but a broken spirit drieth the bones."

Proverbs 17:22

How do we get a merry heart? It starts with the imagination and planting those seeds into your mind, which then begins to root down in your heart. It can't help but erupt out of your mouth when it does. You have to choose to get your mind off of your problems and think on the Word of God. We must realize that the Word of God is positive. It wasn't until I began to meditate on His Word that I began to realize that. I used to think it was boring. I was so wrong. Another way to get yourself happy is to worship! Turn on the worship music and start dancing, even if you don't feel like it. It will get you going, and before you know it, you will really feel it.

"But if the Spirit of him that raised up Jesus from the dead dwell in you, he that raised up Christ from the dead shall also quicken your mortal bodies by his Spirit that dwelleth in you."

Romans 8:11

This is amazing to imagine—the Spirit who raised Jesus from the dead lives in you. He stays in you. He never leaves. Where you go,

He goes. And He loves you like He loves Jesus. As He quickened Jesus, this verse states He will ALSO QUICKEN your mortal body. This means to make alive. Whatever is going on in your body, this verse says He can bring life. You can speak life every day. "The Lord is bringing life to my body as He brought life to Jesus."

"To be carnally minded is death; but to be spiritually minded is life and peace."

Romans 8:6

Think on good things. Keep your mind on things above. Think about Jesus and seeking to get closer to Him and to know Him, for this is our goal. These things bring life and peace. When we are focused on things like unforgiveness, strife, gossip, self-pity, complaining, the lust of the flesh, and such, this all will be sure to bring death—a sure, slow death.

"He giveth power to the faint; and to them that have no might he increaseth strength. Even the youths shall faint and be weary, and the young men shall utterly fall: But they that wait upon the LORD shall renew their strength; they shall mount up with wings as eagles; they shall run, and not be weary; and they shall walk, and not faint."

Isaiah 40:29–31

He gives power to the faint. It comes from Him. When we are weary, we have somewhere to go to be strengthened and refreshed. If you have no might, He will increase your strength. He is able, and if the Word says, "He will do it," then that means He is also willing. It's up to us just to come. Any person on Earth lives in a human body. This means, at some point, we get tired. Even the young get tired, and they are full of youthful energy. But they that wait upon the Lord, no matter what age, will renew their strength. The wingspan of an eagle can be up to eight feet long. They are strong, and the Word often compares the believer to them. The eagle flies high and courageous, never fearing a storm. They know how to handle it. You shall run and not be weary. You shall walk and not faint.

"Surely he hath borne our griefs, and carried our sorrows: yet we did esteem him stricken, smitten of God, and afflicted. But he was wounded for our transgressions, he was bruised for our iniquities: the chastisement of our peace was upon him; and with his stripes we are healed."

Isaiah 53:4–5

Surely. This begins with surely. As they watched, they thought God was punishing Him. Because He had declared He was God, He was being rightfully punished and tortured. They were ignorant of what was really going on. Healing rightfully was paid for us.

"And being not weak in faith, he considered not his own body now dead, when he was about an hundred years old, neither yet the deadness of Sarah's womb: He staggered not at the promise of God through unbelief; but was strong in faith, giving glory to God; And being fully persuaded that, what he had promised,

This is speaking of the journey of Abraham and his faith. How could he be strong in faith even though he had not seen the promise fulfilled? God had promised them a son, but he was old and Sarah was old and barren. He didn't deny the circumstances that were there, but he chose to not consider them. He chose to focus instead on the promise of God. He magnified that promise, and he gave glory to God. This is where he stayed. The more he did this, the stronger his faith became until one day he was fully persuaded. You see, you can get to the point where you believe God, and you know that you know that you know you've got it.

Inside you have this clear picture. And no onecan take it from you. Then, it's just a matter of time before you will see it.

"Now the just shall live by faith:"

Hebrews 10:38

If you are in Christ, you are considered just; you are the righteous ones in Jesus. This is how you should live: by faith—not by what you feel, or what you see, but by faith. We should live by trusting God and taking Him at His Word. He is faithful and true. His Word will never pass away. Isaiah 54:10 says, "For the mountains shall depart, and the hills be removed; but my kindness shall not depart from thee, neither shall the covenant of my peace be removed, saith the LORD that hath mercy on thee."

You please God when you live by faith because that's how He lives. When you live this way, you are saying, "I believe that Jesus paid the full price on the cross for me."

"Beloved, I wish above all things that thou mayest prosper and be in health, even as thy soul prospereth."

3 John 2

He is speaking to believers. If you will read the last part first, that is the key. Your soul must prosper first. What does this mean? The way for a soul to prosper is first to believe in the Son of God and then to be filled with the knowledge of His Word, so much so that it is planted in your heart, growing deep roots. As Psalm 1 says, when you meditate on His Word day and night, the end result will be that you will prosper in all that you do. So as your soul prospers, the rest of your life will also. It begins from the inside out. See a healthy body. See a life that has blossomed in every way.

I pray this book has been an eye opener to the fact that any believer has been given the Word of God to prosper in their soul. Secrets and mysteries are our to unlock, and by the leading of the Holy Spirit, you will set off on an amazing supernatural journey that is part of your rich inheritance from your loving Father that Jesus has provided by His rich grace. Let His Word wash over you, cleansing your thoughts, which in turn bring healing to your mind and your body, and feed your spirit man.

Always know that you are so loved in the kingdom of God!

Linda Patarello

More books by Linda Patarello

The Father Loves

A Worshipper's Heart

How to Meditate on the Living Word Song of Solomon

Purchase on www.heavenstreasures.org and also on Amazon.

About the Author

Linda Patarello is a born again Christian and a graduate of Charis Bible College in Colorado Springs, CO. Linda is a California native and currently lives there, spending most of her time spreading the truth about God's love from the written Word. She also has broad experience leading praise and worship and in songwriting. She believes that the highest calling is to worship the "Giver of All Gifts." She also believes we are born to pursue a relationship with God the Father, Jesus Christ, and the Holy Spirit and to share it with others. Her vision is to help people find true love for the Word of God and to discover for themselves its precious truths that are waiting to be revealed.

For More Information or to Contact the Author, Please Write to:

Heaven's Treasures, P.O. Box 1543 Anaheim, CA 92815 www.heavenstreasures.org